Mind your own GCSE business with CGP!

Doing well in business is all about hard work, determination and giving your customers what they want. The same goes for GCSE Business, except you have to give the examiners what they want. And they're the pickiest customers of all...

Not to worry. This brilliant CGP Revision Guide covers everything you'll need to know for the Grade 9-1 Edexcel course, from enterprise to e-commerce.

We've also included plenty of practice questions and top advice to help you score market-leading results in the exams!

CGP — still the best! ☺

Our sole aim here at CGP is to produce the highest quality books — carefully written, immaculately presented and dangerously close to being funny.

Then we work our socks off to get them out to you — at the cheapest possible prices.

Contents

Published by CGP

Based on the classic CGP style created by Richard Parsons

Editors: Charlotte Burrows, Emily Howe, Duncan Lindsay, Ciara McGlade and Rachael Rogers.
Contributor: Colin Harber-Stuart

ISBN: 978 1 78294 690 8

With thanks to Rachel Kordan and Victoria Skelton for the proofreading.

With thanks to Ana Pungartnik for the copyright research.

Page 9 contains public sector information licensed under the Open Government Licence v3.0.
http://www.nationalarchives.gov.uk/doc/open-government-licence/version/3/

Pages 11 and 34 contain information from the Office for National Statistics licensed under the Open Government Licence v3.0.
http://www.nationalarchives.gov.uk/doc/open-government-licence/version/3/

Google Pay is a trademark of Google LLC and this book is not endorsed by or affiliated with Google in any way.

Every effort has been made to locate copyright holders and obtain permission to reproduce sources. For those sources where it has been difficult to trace the originator of the work, we would be grateful for information. If any copyright holder would like us to make an amendment to the acknowledgements, please notify us and we will gladly update the book at the next reprint. Thank you.

Printed by Elanders Ltd, Newcastle upon Tyne.
Clipart from Corel®

Enterprise

Businesses don't <u>only</u> exist so that you can take a GCSE in Business... They provide lots of other <u>useful</u> things as well. Like chocolate, stationery, or the purple velvet hat I bought last week.

Businesses Wouldn't Exist Without Enterprise

1) <u>Business enterprise</u> is the process of <u>identifying</u> new business opportunities, and then <u>taking advantage</u> of them. It can involve starting up a <u>new business</u>, or helping an <u>existing one</u> to <u>expand</u> by coming up with <u>new ideas</u>.

2) All <u>business activity</u> needs to have at least one <u>purpose</u>. A purpose could be to:

- Provide people with a <u>good</u> (a physical item such as a book or furniture) or a <u>service</u> (an action performed by other people to aid the customer, such as hairdressing or plumbing).

  A 'product' can be a good or a service.

- Meet <u>customer needs</u> — this means providing goods and services that people will <u>want to buy</u>. Customer needs often <u>change</u> so firms may need to change the products they sell to keep up.

- <u>Add value</u> to an existing product — this means a business finds a way to <u>improve</u> a product, so customers are willing to <u>pay more</u> for it compared to competitors' products. There are <u>several ways</u> a business can add value to a product. For example, it could:

  - make a product <u>more convenient</u> for customers to <u>get</u> or <u>use</u> (e.g. a <u>mobile</u> hairdresser might be more convenient for customers than having to visit a hairdresser's <u>salon</u>).

  - build a good <u>brand image</u> for a product (see p.54) — customers will be more willing to spend money on the product as they'll <u>recognise</u> the brand and know that it's <u>trustworthy</u> and <u>desirable</u>.

  - improve the product's <u>design</u> or <u>quality</u>.

  - give the product a <u>unique selling point</u> (USP). This is some <u>feature</u> that makes it different from its <u>competitors</u>, which makes it an <u>original</u> product.

New Business Ideas Come About for a Variety of Reasons

1) The world we live in is always <u>changing</u>, and so businesses must be <u>dynamic</u> and <u>adapt</u> to these changes.

2) This often results in people coming up with <u>new business ideas</u>.

- Many new business ideas come about from <u>changes</u> in <u>technology</u>. For example, the invention of <u>tablets</u> meant lots of people came up with ideas for <u>apps</u> that could be used on these devices.

- Some business ideas come about because of changes in <u>what customers want</u>. For example, these days people are much more concerned about <u>the environment</u>, so many businesses have started up that offer more <u>environmentally friendly</u> products.

- Sometimes, a <u>good or service</u> becomes <u>obsolete</u> — this means it's <u>no longer used</u>, usually because it has become <u>out-dated</u> and has been <u>replaced</u> by something else. Business owners have to come up with <u>new ideas</u> so that their business <u>survives</u>. E.g. as <u>DVDs</u> became obsolete, some DVD rental companies began offering <u>subscription streaming services</u> in order to survive.

3) New business ideas will either be completely <u>original</u> (there hasn't been anything like it before) or an <u>adaptation</u> of an <u>existing product or idea</u> (but the business will have found a way to <u>improve</u> it or make it <u>more relevant</u> to customers at the time).

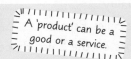

In the 1970s, James Dyson came up with the idea of a <u>vacuum cleaner</u> that didn't need <u>dust bags</u>. <u>Customers</u> wanted to buy the vacuum cleaner, as it meant they no longer had to <u>buy</u> replacement bags and the new vacuum cleaner didn't lose <u>suction</u>.

Let's get down to business...

Well that wasn't too bad. Make sure you know what businesses are for and why people come up with business ideas.

More on Enterprise

Running a business can be risky, and hard hats and high vis jackets are unlikely to make things easier. But if everything goes well, the rewards of running a successful business can be worth all the stress.

Entrepreneurs *Take Advantage of Business Opportunities*

1) An entrepreneur is someone who takes on the risks of enterprise activity.

2) Entrepreneurs are really important — without them, we'd never have any new businesses.

3) To successfully run a new business, an entrepreneur must be able to:

- Organise resources — entrepreneurs have to have good organisational skills to keep on top of all the day-to-day tasks of running the business as well as planning for the future. E.g. they have to make sure the business has all the right resources (such as money and supplies) at the right time.

- Take risks — there are lots of unknowns involved in running a business. The entrepreneur will probably give up their current job and invest money that they could lose if the business fails. They can write a business plan to work out if the business is a good idea (see p.26), but they can't know exactly what's going to happen before they start, so they have to be willing to take calculated risks.

- Make business decisions — there are lots of decisions that need to be made when running a business, and not all of them are easy to make. For example, the entrepreneur needs to be able to decide on the business's aims, its structure, who to employ, how to grow and what to do if things start going wrong.

There are *Risks* and *Rewards* in Running a Business

Risks

1) To start a business, an entrepreneur needs money to buy equipment and pay workers. An entrepreneur will often use their own money, but they'll probably need to raise more from banks or other investors as well (see p.18). If the business makes a financial loss, it won't be able to pay back all the money that's been borrowed (and it may struggle to survive).

2) Entrepreneurs don't have much security when they are starting a new business. They'll usually have given up another job to follow their business idea, and if things go wrong they could lose money and end up without any job, which could have a huge impact on their quality of life.

3) There's always a risk that a business will fail. So the entrepreneur risks the money, time and effort they put in to trying to make the business work.

Rewards

1) For many entrepreneurs, one big reward is seeing their business idea become a success.

2) If the business makes lots of profit, the entrepreneur could earn more money than they did before they started the business. This could give them a better quality of life.

3) Being an entrepreneur can also be rewarding as it gives the entrepreneur the independence to choose what they do day-to-day, and what direction the business goes in.

Be careful of the baking industry — it's full of whisks...

For many entrepreneurs the road to success can be very long and wobbly. Make sure you know the roles of an entrepreneur, the risks they face and the rewards they can enjoy if their business dreams come true.

Competition

The business world isn't one of those friendly 'it's the taking part that counts' types of competition. Oh, no. Rival businesses will work as hard as they can to beat their competitors.

A Market can be a Place, a Product or a Group of People

The word market can mean three slightly different things:

1) A place where goods are traded between customers and suppliers. A village market square seems pretty different from an internet shopping website — but they're both examples of markets.

2) Trade in a particular type of product, e.g. the oil market.

3) The potential customers for a product, e.g. the age 18–25 market.

Competitors are the different businesses that sell the same products in the same market. They compete with each other over sales to customers.

Competition Affects How Businesses Make Decisions

1) Most businesses face competition. To stand out in a competitive environment, businesses need to make decisions that will persuade customers to buy from them, rather than their competitors.

2) When making these decisions, the business might look at the strengths and weaknesses of its competitors in the following areas:

1) **Price** — Customers will often want to pay less for a given product. If all the products in the market are the same, then price becomes one of the most important factors affecting which products customers will buy. Therefore firms may decide to charge lower prices than they would like, to stop customers from buying elsewhere. However, this will mean that a firm may not make much profit per product sold.

2) **Customer service** — Offering customer service can attract customers and may mean that customers will be willing to pay more money for a product (and having a reputation for poor customer service might put customers off). So to stand out from the competition, a business might decide to train its staff in good customer service, or provide extra services (such as user training) when the customer buys the product.

3) **Quality** — Offering better quality products may mean that customers are more satisfied. This may mean that the business will be more competitive, even if its products are more expensive. In order to convince customers that their products are better than their rivals', businesses may decide to spend money on developing high quality products or on promotional material that emphasises quality. However, this will be costly for the firm.

4) **Product range** — Having a large range of products may make a business more attractive to customers. E.g. a greengrocers may be able to compete with a convenience store if it sells more types of fruit and vegetables, since customers will have a better selection in one place. A business may also try to fill any gap in the market (supply a previously unmet consumer need) by developing new products. There won't be any competition for the new products and the firm may appear more innovative than its competitors and so be more attractive to customers.

5) **Location** — Customers may be more likely to buy from a business if it sells products in a convenient place as they won't have the inconvenience of travelling or waiting for the product. Therefore businesses may decide to open stores in particular locations or to sell items online in order to offer the greatest convenience to customers as possible.

I'm not competitive — I just really don't like losing...

PRACTICE QUESTION

Q1 State and explain the level of competition you think that a shop selling clothes on a local high street would face.

Q2 Give two ways in which a business selling poor quality goods may be able to stay competitive.

Introduction to Market Research

Market research involves <u>finding out</u> what customers want (what they really, really want)...

It's Useful For Businesses to Understand Markets

1) Businesses sometimes carry out market research in order to find out about the <u>market</u> (see previous page) and how they are <u>performing</u> in it.

2) For example, they may want to know the overall <u>market size</u> and the business's <u>market share</u>.

3) The <u>market size</u> is the number of individuals (including companies) within the market which are <u>potential buyers</u> or <u>sellers</u> of products. It can also mean the <u>total value</u> of <u>products</u> in the market.

4) The <u>market share</u> of a business is the <u>proportion</u> of total sales within the market that is controlled by the <u>business</u>.

5) As well as understanding the business's <u>place</u> in a market, it's also important for the business to carry out market research into its <u>customers</u>.

Market Research is Used to Understand Customers

1) All businesses need their customers to <u>buy</u> their products, otherwise they <u>won't survive</u>.

2) One purpose of market research is to <u>identify</u> who the business's customers <u>are</u>. They can use <u>market segmentation</u> to help them do this (see p.8).

3) Market research can then be used to give businesses an <u>understanding</u> of their customers — e.g. what their <u>needs</u> are and how to <u>satisfy</u> them.

4) Customers' needs may include things like: the <u>type</u> of product, the <u>quality</u> of a product, the <u>price</u>, the <u>convenience</u> of where it is sold and how much <u>choice</u> they have of a range of products (e.g. different colours or sizes).

5) By understanding customers' needs, businesses will be better able to make products that <u>meet</u> these needs. This will <u>increase</u> their <u>sales</u> and help to ensure the business's <u>survival</u>.

Market Research Helps to Improve Businesses

Using market research to understand customers and their needs helps businesses to:

Make informed decisions

Market research provides useful information to businesses to help them decide things like:

- <u>what</u> products to sell
- <u>where to sell them</u> and how to <u>promote</u> them
- <u>what price</u> to sell them for

Spot a gap in the market

1) Sometimes a group of customers will have a need that <u>isn't being met</u>. This is a <u>gap in the market</u>. A business will want to develop a way to meet the customers' needs before its <u>competitors</u> do.

2) This might mean developing a <u>new product</u>. Or it might mean selling an existing product in a <u>new place</u> or at a <u>new price</u>, or <u>promoting</u> it in a new way to convince customers they need it.

Reduce risks

1) If a business sells a product that customers <u>don't want</u> or tries to sell products at a price that's <u>too high</u> or in the <u>wrong location</u>, it could end up <u>losing</u> a lot of money.

2) Using market research to make <u>informed decisions</u> will help the business to <u>avoid</u> this and therefore help to <u>reduce</u> the risk of making <u>costly mistakes</u>.

My market research involves the fudge stall, bakery, crêperie...

Customers are so needy, which is great news for businesses — get it right and they'll make money, money, money...

Types of Market Research

You can have primary or secondary market research — you need to know about both types, so get reading...

Primary Research *is Doing Your Own Donkey Work*

1) Primary research involves getting information from customers or potential customers.

2) Most forms of primary research involve asking customers for their opinions.
   For example, questionnaires (documents with questions that are given to people), surveys (collecting information from people, e.g. directly over the phone or using questionnaires) and focus groups (where a small group of people discuss their attitudes towards a product).

3) Observation involves (you've guessed it) observing what people do or say, instead of asking them.

4) Primary research is useful for finding out new information, and getting customers' views.

5) But a business can't ask every potential customer for their views — usually just a sample of people.

6) Large samples are the most accurate but also the most expensive. Small businesses may have to compromise here and use small sample groups to keep their costs down.

7) Businesses can also save on costs by carrying out research over the telephone or internet rather than in person — this is especially useful for small businesses.

8) Primary research provides data that's up-to-date, relevant and specific to the needs of your business. The research can also be specific to the target market.

9) But on the downside, it's expensive, and can be time-consuming.

10) Different types of primary research have different advantages and disadvantages.
    E.g. observations are really cheap and give accurate information, but also don't allow customers to give opinions — so the business will know what customers are doing, but not necessarily the reasons why. Questionnaires are cheap and can be used to sample a large geographic area, but it's likely that many people won't respond. Phone surveys have a much higher rate of response but they can be more expensive. Focus groups are faster than surveying several people individually, but may mean that quieter individuals do not get their opinion heard.

Secondary Research *is Looking at Other People's Work*

1) Secondary research allows access to a wide range of data — not just the views of their sample groups. It's useful for looking at the whole market, and analysing past trends to predict the future.

2) It involves looking at things like market research reports, government reports, and articles in newspapers and magazines and on the internet.

3) It's often used by small businesses as it's cheaper than primary research, and the data is easily found and instantly available.

4) Disadvantages of secondary research are that it's not always relevant to your needs, it's not specifically about your products, and it's often out of date.

Social Media *Can be Used for Market Research*

1) Social media includes websites such as Facebook® and Twitter. These sorts of sites allow people to create profiles of themselves on the internet. That includes putting the things that they enjoy.

2) Businesses can sometimes collect this information and use it for their market research. For example, they can see what sorts of things are popular or are increasing in popularity.

Telephone surveys — don't get hung up about them...

Market research is crucial for new businesses — they need to decide what they want to find out about the market and then choose the best method for collecting the data. Or things could go belly-up pretty quickly.

Using Market Research

Market research data can be used to see if a business has any problems or how it might improve. It's important to collect the right kind of data, though, and to have data that's reliable. No pressure...

Data Can be Quantitative or Qualitative

Ohhh... sweeeet... cheesy... nom nom nom...

I'm sorry — what was the question again?

1) Suppose you want to do some market research about chocolate pizza. You can find out two kinds of information.

2) Quantitative information is anything you can measure or reduce to a number. Asking "How many chocolate pizzas will you buy each week?" will give a quantitative answer.

3) Qualitative information is all about people's feelings and opinions. Asking "What do you think of chocolate pizzas?" will give a qualitative answer. Qualitative data is tricky to analyse because it's hard to compare two people's opinions. However, allowing customers to voice their opinions is likely to give a greater depth of information.

4) Good market research will use both types of information.

5) All market research data needs to be reliable — this means that its results can be repeated by another researcher. Reliable market research represents the people that the business is interested in accurately. The more reliable the data is, the more useful it is for a business.

You Need to be Able to Interpret Market Research

You can use the results of market research to inform decisions a business should make — such as ideas about the products it sells, how it promotes itself, its pricing or the place it sells its products — these things are all part of the marketing mix (see p.24). For example:

BUSINESS EXAMPLE

1) 'Crazy Juice Ltd' wanted customers' views of their damson juice. They sent a questionnaire to 2000 of their existing customers.

2) The collected data is shown on the right. An analysis of this data could look something like this:

'The results show that more than a quarter of the sample group have made a trial purchase of damson juice. This shows that the company's advertising for the product is successfully attracting customers. However, very few of these customers go on to make repeat purchases. This suggests that there is a problem with the product itself. Crazy Juice Ltd need to consider changing the product, or dropping it altogether.'

Q1a: How many times have you purchased damson juice?

Never	1290
Once	580
Twice	80
Three times	40
Four or more times	10

Q1b: If you answered 'once', would you buy it again?

Yes	60
No	520

3) These pie charts show the results of Crazy Juice Ltd's research into why people buy their products, carried out in 1992 and 2016.

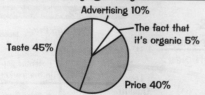
Reasons for buying Crazy Juice — 1992
Advertising 10%, The fact that it's organic 5%, Taste 45%, Price 40%

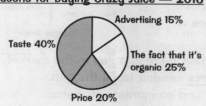
Reasons for buying Crazy Juice — 2016
Advertising 15%, The fact that it's organic 25%, Taste 40%, Price 20%

4) An analysis of the charts would include points like...
- Taste was the most important factor in both years.
- More people bought Crazy Juice because it's organic in 2016 than in 1992.
- Price decreased in importance from 1992 to 2016.

5) Because of this research, Crazy Juice might change their promotional material to emphasise the taste and environmental friendliness of the drink.

6) It's important that the quality of the product stays the same, but price has become less important to customers, so it might be possible to increase the price of the drink, without decreasing sales by too much.

Sales analysis — go on, try it. You might like it...

Q1 Write whether the following types of data are quantitative or qualitative:
a) sales figures for different products, b) reports on the quality of products from customers.

Market Segmentation

Segmenting a market can help a business to figure out who exactly they are most interested in selling to. They can also use market research data to create a market map so that they can really zone in on what other products are out there, and what they need to do to increase sales. Get ready for more market magic...

Markets are Segmented into Different Groups of People

1) As well as knowing market size and shares (p.5) it can be useful to know how a market is segmented.

2) Segmentation is when people within a market are divided into different groups.

3) Knowing the different market segments can allow businesses to identify their target market — this is the specific group of people that a product is aimed at (see below).

4) They can then create a marketing strategy aimed at their target market (a targeted marketing strategy) to make sure that their marketing is as effective as possible.

> Marketing is all about coming up with a product that people will buy, and then making it as easy as possible for them to buy it — see p.24 for more.

5) A market can be segmented by its demographics. These are identifiable characteristics that people within one population might have. For example:

- Age — for example the teenage market, or "grey power" (the over-55s).
- Income — how much different people earn will affect what they are willing to buy.

6) But demographics isn't the only way to segment a market. Other ways include:

- Location — try selling stottie cakes outside the North East, or jellied eels outside London.
- Lifestyle — whether or not people enjoy certain activities, e.g. walking, cycling or reading.

We're targeting London-based Geordies. Jellied stottie eel cakes

Businesses Map the Market to Find Information

1) Mapping the market helps a business understand its location within the market, and the market's key features. Market maps are often in the form of a diagram (see below).

2) A business can use a market map to find out the following bits of information:

- Competitors selling similar products — and how customers perceive them.
- Any gaps in the market — see p.5.

3) Market maps like the one on the right show two variables — in this case, price and quality, but they could be almost anything.

4) The map allows a business to see how customers perceive key features of its competitors' products — e.g. their pricing and quality strategies.

5) They can also easily see if there is any part of the map with no products — i.e. a potential gap in the market.

6) Once they have spotted a potential gap in the market, the business will need to use market research to confirm whether or not there is demand for the type of product which they have identified.

7) If they identify that there is demand for this type of product, then there is a gap in the market. So the business can focus on creating products with the features needed to fill the gap. This will help the business to be different from the competition and so increase its sales.

Market Map for Instant Coffee
Premium Price — Mountain Grind, Full-o-Beans, Supercharge, potential gap in the market, Get Me Up, Roast Away, Brown and Dirty, Café Toujours, Low Quality / High Quality, Budget Price

I love segments — of a certain type of chocolate orange...

Businesses can't succeed without understanding their place in the market. They need to know who their customers are, what they need, and whether these needs are being met by the competition. One up for market research.

Case Study — Topics 1.1 & 1.2

That's almost it for Spotting a Business Opportunity, but first here's a lovely case study to bring everything together. Before you start, have a look back at Topic 1.1 as well. Trust me, it'll help you.

Business Report: Enterprise, Entrepreneurship and Spotting a Business Opportunity

Cycling Clothing

Ankita enjoys cycling, and has noticed an increase in the number of people who cycle regularly. She is considering leaving her current job and setting up a business making clothing for cyclists. Ankita would aim to develop a strong brand image for her company through selling clothing that is well designed and comfortable. She is considering whether to target people who cycle to commute, or people who cycle to race.

Ankita does some internet research and finds that the percentage of people cycling to work increased from 2.8% to 4% between 2011 and 2015. She also sends out a survey to people at her work and asks anyone who cycles to respond. The survey asks how people perceive existing companies who provide clothing for cyclists. From the results of this survey, she produces the market map shown on the right. In the survey, she also asks the cyclists why they cycle, and to describe what they look for when buying cycling clothes. From this, she finds that 73% of the respondents only cycle to commute and that they prioritise how fashionable the clothing is. 20% of the respondents also attend cycling races, so are more interested in having high performance clothing.

Market map:
Fashion-Focused Design
- Dynamic
- Bart's Bikes
Low Performance — High Performance
- Free Wheeler
- Saeed's Cycles
- Gear Shift
- HUW Sports
- Push the Pedal
Regular Design

Case Study Questions

One case study, questions from two topics. Better get cracking.

1) Explain why Ankita has come up with a business idea.
2) Explain how Ankita will add value to her cycling clothing.
3) Explain one benefit to Ankita of carrying out market research.
4) What type of market research is Ankita conducting by doing internet research?
5) Using the market research data above, explain whether Ankita should target people who cycle to commute or people who cycle to race.

I want to ride my bicycle, I want to ride it where I like...

Make sure you've answered all the questions for this case study. The trick is to use details from the case study in your answer. Once you're happy with each of your answers, have a go at the questions on the next page...

Revision Summary — Topics 1.1 & 1.2

There you go, a little bit on why people start up businesses and then some of the research that they can do to make sure their business idea is sound. Now, time for some questions to see how you're doing so far.

1) What is enterprise?
2) Give three purposes of business activity.
3) Explain why a firm might try to make a product more convenient for the customer.
4) What does USP stand for?
5) Explain three reasons why new business ideas come about.
6) What is an entrepreneur?
7) List three things an entrepreneur must be able to do in order to run a successful business.
8) Explain three rewards an entrepreneur might get from setting up a business.
9) Describe three meanings of the term 'market'.
10) List five areas where a business may compare itself to its competitors.
11) Describe two factors about a business that can make it stand out from its competition.
12) Why is it important for a business to understand a customer's needs?
13) Give two customer needs that a business might want to identify.
14) Give three types of business decisions which may be informed by a business's market research.
15) Explain how market research can help a business to reduce its risks.
16) What is the main difference between primary market research and secondary market research?
17) Give four methods of primary market research.
18) Give two methods of secondary market research.
19) Would a small firm be more likely to use primary or secondary market research? Explain your answer.
20) Give one example of how a business may use social media for its market research.
21) What is the difference between quantitative and qualitative market research?
22) What is meant by reliable market research?
23) Why might a firm want to segment a market when conducting market research?
24) Give four different ways of segmenting a market.
25) Give two pieces of information which a business might find out from a market map.

Business Aims and Objectives

Businesses need to have <u>aims</u> — overall <u>goals</u> that they want to achieve. They also need <u>objectives</u>, which are like <u>mini aims</u> (there's more on these on the next page). Aims and objectives can be <u>financial</u> or <u>non-financial</u>.

Financial Aims *Can be Measured in Terms of Money*

Survival

Around <u>60%</u> of new firms close within five years of starting, so just <u>surviving</u> is the main and most important <u>short-term</u> aim of all new businesses. This means the business needs to have <u>enough money</u> to stay open, e.g. to buy <u>stock</u> and pay <u>staff</u>.

Maximise Profit

The vast majority of firms will aim to <u>maximise profits</u>. However, it may take a few years for a new firm to make any profit at all.

Increase Market Share

Market share tells you what <u>percentage</u> of a market's <u>total sales</u> a particular product or company has made. When a business first starts up it has zero market share... so one of its first aims is to capture a part of the market and <u>establish</u> itself. It can then aim to increase its market share by taking sales <u>away</u> from competition, or by persuading <u>new customers</u> to enter the market and buy its products.

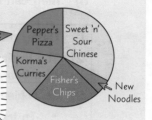

Sweet 'n Sour Chinese has a big market share already, but New Noodles might want to try and increase its share of the market.

Maximise Sales

Increasing <u>sales</u> is a good way for a business to grow its <u>market share</u>. The business can monitor sales in terms of <u>how many</u> of a particular product it sells, or by how <u>much money</u> it takes in from selling its products. This is not the same as maximising <u>profit</u>. For example, a business might <u>reduce prices</u> in order to increase sales, but selling products <u>more cheaply</u> means it won't make as much <u>profit</u> (see page 13).

Achieve Financial Security

Many businesses will depend on <u>external sources of finance</u> such as <u>loans</u> or the business owners' <u>personal savings</u> when they first start. So an aim for a <u>new business</u> is likely to be achieving a point where it can depend on its <u>own revenue</u> to fund its activities (i.e. its sales go beyond its <u>break-even point</u> — see p.14).

There May be *Non-Financial Aims* for Starting a Business

Many new businesses have aims that <u>aren't</u> centred around <u>money</u>. These aims include:

1) Accomplishing a <u>personal challenge</u> — some people want the <u>challenge</u> of setting up and running a new business. And if the risks pay off, there could be big <u>rewards</u> (see p.3).

2) Achieving <u>personal satisfaction</u> — some people want the <u>satisfaction</u> that comes with owning their own business, particularly if their company allows them to follow an <u>interest</u>. E.g. a <u>history-lover</u> might set up a <u>tour company</u> for a historical site. Being <u>interested</u> in what they do can a give a person a lot of <u>job satisfaction</u>.

3) Gaining <u>independence and control</u> — some people might want the <u>independence</u> of being their own <u>boss</u>. This means they have <u>control</u> over what they <u>do</u> each day, and make the decisions about <u>how</u> the business will be run. They might have <u>flexible working hours</u>, meaning it's easier to fit <u>work</u> around <u>other commitments</u>, like <u>childcare</u>.

4) Doing what's right for <u>society</u> — some firms want to make sure they are acting in ways that are <u>best for society</u> and that society believes are <u>morally right</u> (e.g. many consumers think that it's <u>wrong</u> to test cosmetics on animals).

Survival — also the main aim during exam time...

Having aims is important for a business. Managers use aims to make decisions about how the business should be run. And having aims means anyone interested in the business can easily work out what the business is all about.

More on Business Aims and Objectives

Aims can be pretty <u>vague</u> and <u>overwhelming</u> for a business. Luckily, objectives mean aims can be broken down into <u>bitesized chunks</u>. So suddenly, things don't seem so <u>scary</u> anymore.

Objectives *Help Businesses* Achieve *Their Aims*

1) Once a firm has established its aims, it needs to set business <u>objectives</u>.

2) Just like with aims, there are different <u>types</u> of objectives. They can be related to survival, profit, market share, sales, financial security, personal reasons or social issues.

3) Objectives are more <u>specific</u> than aims — they're <u>measurable</u> steps on the way to the aim. E.g. if a firm's aim is to <u>maximise sales</u>, an objective might be to increase income from sales by <u>30%</u> over <u>two years</u>.

4) Once objectives have been set they act as <u>clear targets</u> for firms to work towards.

5) They can then be used later to <u>measure</u> whether a firm has been <u>successful</u> or not.

> BUSINESS EXAMPLE
>
> 1) Cathy owns a <u>bike hire</u> business.
>
> 2) The business has a <u>social aim</u> to <u>improve the fitness</u> of <u>primary school children</u> in the local area.
>
> 3) To achieve this aim, Cathy sets the following <u>objectives</u>:
> - To <u>train two volunteers</u> to teach children how to ride a bike.
> - To work with a local <u>primary school</u> to offer an <u>after-school cycle club</u>.
> - To teach <u>30 children</u> to ride a bike during the <u>first school year</u> of the project.
> - To speak to her <u>local councillor</u> about setting up a <u>cycle path</u> in the local park.
>
> 4) After a year, she can <u>look back</u> and see how well these objectives have been <u>achieved</u>. She can then <u>adjust</u> them if necessary in order to continue working towards her <u>aim</u>.

Not All *Companies Have the* Same Aims *and* Objectives

There are <u>different factors</u> that affect the aims and objectives of a business. For example:

1) The <u>size</u> and <u>age</u> of the business — many <u>small</u> and <u>new</u> businesses are likely to focus on <u>survival</u> and <u>growth</u>. As firms <u>grow</u> and become <u>more established</u> they may concentrate more on achieving <u>financial security</u>, and <u>increasing sales</u> and <u>market share</u>. <u>Larger</u> businesses get more <u>attention</u> from the public, so they might set <u>social</u> aims and objectives to try to avoid bad publicity.

2) Who <u>owns</u> the business — for small businesses that are owned by only <u>one</u> or a <u>small number</u> of people (e.g. sole traders and partnerships — see p.21), <u>non-financial</u> aims and objectives such as achieving <u>personal satisfaction</u> may be more important than growing sales or market share, especially when the business is still <u>young</u>. For companies that are owned by many <u>shareholders</u> (e.g. private limited companies — see p.22) there may be pressure to have aims and objectives focused on <u>maximising profit</u> so shareholders get <u>more money</u>.

3) The <u>level of competition</u> the business faces — if a business is in a <u>highly competitive</u> market, it might focus on <u>survival</u> or <u>maximising sales</u>. If a firm doesn't face much competition, its aims and objectives may be focused more on <u>increasing market share</u> and <u>maximising profits</u>.

> PRACTICE QUESTION
>
> ### *You may object, but you've still got to learn all this...*
>
> Q1 Green Machines is a small firm that makes lawnmowers. It has been running for three years and currently its main aim is to maximise its profits.
>
> a) Identify how Green Machines could use objectives to help it achieve its aim.
>
> b) A new, competitor firm that makes lawnmowers has recently been set up.
> Explain how the aims of the competitor firm may differ from Green Machines' aims.

Revenue, Cost and Profit

You won't be given the <u>equations</u> on this page in your exam — so make sure you learn them <u>off by heart</u>.

Revenue *is the Income Earned by a Business*

1) Businesses earn most of their <u>income</u> from <u>selling</u> their products to customers.

2) Revenue can be <u>calculated</u> by multiplying <u>quantity</u> of units <u>sold</u> by the <u>price</u> (the amount the customer pays).

> **BUSINESS EXAMPLE**
> revenue = quantity sold × price

> If Britney's Spheres Ltd. sell <u>20 000</u> tennis balls at <u>£2</u> each — their <u>sales revenue</u> will be <u>£40 000</u>.

Costs *are the Expenses Paid Out to Run the Business*

1) <u>Fixed</u> costs <u>don't vary</u> with output (the amount a business produces). They <u>have to be paid</u> even if the firm produces <u>nothing</u>. For example, the <u>rent</u>, <u>insurance</u>, <u>fixed salaries</u> for employees and <u>advertising</u>.

2) <u>Variable</u> costs are costs that will <u>increase</u> as the firm <u>expands output</u>. For example, the costs of <u>factory labour</u>, <u>raw materials</u> and <u>running machinery</u>.

> total variable cost = quantity sold × variable cost per unit

3) Fixed costs are only fixed over a <u>short period</u> of time — an expanding firm's fixed costs will go up.

4) The <u>total costs</u> for a firm are the <u>fixed</u> and <u>variable</u> costs <u>added together</u>:

> total costs = total variable costs + total fixed costs

Interest *is Added to Loans and Savings*

1) When a business <u>borrows</u> money, it will usually have to pay it back with <u>interest</u> — this is a <u>charge</u> for borrowing money. So the business will pay back <u>more</u> than was borrowed.

2) Interest can be written as a <u>percentage</u> of the original amount borrowed. To find the amount of interest that a business has paid on a loan just use the following <u>equation</u>:

> interest (on loans) = $\dfrac{\text{total repayment} - \text{borrowed amount}}{\text{borrowed amount}} \times 100$

> Britney's Spheres Ltd. took out a loan of <u>£10 000</u>. It paid off the loan and interest to a total of <u>£10 800</u>. So interest on the loan was <u>8%</u>.
>
> **BUSINESS EXAMPLE**
>
> Interest = $\dfrac{10\ 800 - 10\ 000}{10\ 000} \times 100$
> = (800 ÷ 10 000) × 100 = 8%

You can calculate the total repayment by multiplying the monthly repayment by the number of months the firm is taking to repay the loan.

3) Interest is also <u>added on</u> to <u>savings</u>. So a business can also <u>earn money</u> through interest on savings.

Businesses Make a *Profit if They Earn More Than They Spend*

<u>Profit</u> (or loss) is the difference between revenue and costs over a <u>period of time</u>.

> profit = revenue − costs

> Britney's Spheres Ltd. sells <u>20 000</u> tennis balls in a month at <u>£2 each</u>. Over the same month its total costs are <u>£30 000</u>.
> Profit = (20 000 × £2) − £30 000 = £40 000 − £30 000 = £10 000
> So the business makes <u>£10 000 profit</u> in the month.
>
> **BUSINESS EXAMPLE**

Sounds like a load of balls to me.

If <u>costs</u> are <u>higher</u> than revenue, the business will make a <u>loss</u> instead of a profit, and the answer to the calculation above will be <u>negative</u>.

> **PRACTICE QUESTION**
>
> ### Interest is to savings what sprinkles are to ice cream — mmm...
>
> Q1 Gnome Bargains make garden gnomes. The total cost of producing 5000 gnomes is £12 500. Each gnome is sold for £7. Calculate the profit Gnome Bargains will make if they sell all 5000 gnomes.

Break-Even Analysis

Break-even analysis allows firms to find out the minimum amount they need to sell to get by. I know what you're thinking — trust me it's not a good strategy for revision...

Breaking Even *Means Covering Your Costs*

1) The break-even level of output or break-even point is the level of sales (or output) a firm needs in order to just cover its costs.

2) It can be measured by the number of units a firm needs to sell to break-even:

3) Or it can be measured by the revenue the firm needs to make to cover its costs:

$$\text{break-even point in units} = \frac{\text{fixed cost}}{\text{sales price} - \text{variable cost}}$$

This is the variable cost per unit.

break-even point for revenue (or costs) = break-even point in units × sales price

4) If a firm sells more than the break-even point, it'll make a profit — if it sells less, it'll make a loss.

5) New businesses should always do a break-even analysis to find the break-even level of output.

> BUSINESS EXAMPLE
> - Pin-Chit Ltd. make padlocks. They have fixed costs of £2000, and the variable cost per unit is £2. The selling price is £4.
> - Their break-even output = 2000 ÷ (4 – 2) = 2000 ÷ 2 = 1000 units
> - So the firm will break even if it makes and sells 1000 units.
> - The break-even point for revenue = 1000 × 4 = £4000
> - This means that the firm should have a revenue of £4000 in order to break even.

6) A low break-even output is good for a business as it won't have to sell as much to make a profit.

Break-even Diagrams *Show the Effect of Output* Changing

A break-even diagram has number of sales or output on the x-axis, and costs and revenues on the y-axis.

To find the break-even point for costs or revenue, find the point at which the line for total costs crosses the line for total revenue. Then draw a line across to the y-axis and read off the value.

The difference between the total costs and the total revenue at any point on the graph tells you the profit (or loss) a firm will make at that level of output.

The total revenue increases as more units are sold.

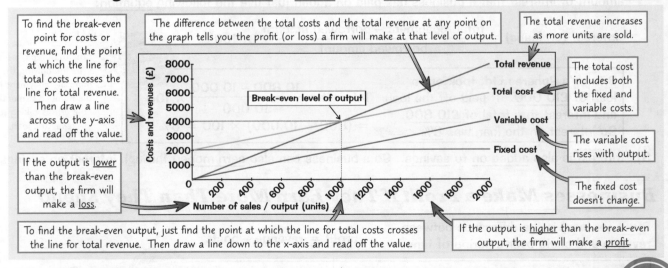

The total cost includes both the fixed and variable costs.

The variable cost rises with output.

The fixed cost doesn't change.

If the output is lower than the break-even output, the firm will make a loss.

To find the break-even output, just find the point at which the line for total costs crosses the line for total revenue. Then draw a line down to the x-axis and read off the value.

If the output is higher than the break-even output, the firm will make a profit.

> BUSINESS EXAMPLE
> The break-even diagram above is for Pin-Chit Ltd. You can see that:
> - Fixed costs are £2000. Variable costs increase £2 for every unit sold. So, total costs start at £2000 and increase £2 for every unit sold.
> - Total revenue rises £4 for each unit sold (since the price of each padlock is £4).
> - The break-even level of output is 1000 units or £4000.
> - Total costs (and variable costs) are rising at a slower rate than revenue. So, as output increases, profit per unit also increases.

Always cover your costs — for example, sweep 'em under the rug...

Ideally, businesses would make a profit all the time, but if it's not possible then breaking even is the next best thing.

More on Break-Even Analysis

Even more on break-even analysis here (yay) — this time, how to find the <u>margin of safety</u> for a given level of output. This is an easy way of seeing how much a business's output can <u>fall</u> before it starts making a <u>loss</u>.

You Need to be Able to Find the Margin of Safety

1) The <u>margin of safety</u> for a firm is the <u>gap</u> between the <u>current</u> level of output and the <u>break-even output</u>.

2) You can find the margin of safety using the following <u>equation</u>:

> margin of safety = actual sales (or budgeted sales) – break-even sales

Firms forecast how much they are likely to sell in a given period of time. These predictions are often based on previous sales and their best guess.

3) The firm will use budgeted sales if it is trying to <u>forecast</u> its future margin of safety. The budgeted sales will be the sales that it <u>expects</u> to make.

> **BUSINESS EXAMPLE**
>
> 1) Pin-Chit Ltd. need to sell <u>1000 units</u> in order to <u>break even</u> (see previous page).
> 2) In one financial year, the company sold <u>1800 units</u>.
> 3) The <u>margin of safety</u> for the company was therefore 1800 – 1000 = <u>800 units</u>.
> 4) This means that the firm's output would have to <u>fall</u> by <u>800 units</u> the next year before it would start to make a <u>loss</u>.
> 5) You can also show Pin-Chit Ltd.'s margin of safety using a <u>break-even diagram</u>:
>
>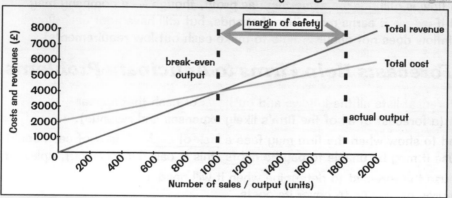

Revenue and Costs May Change

1) Break-even diagrams can also be useful for seeing how <u>changes</u> in <u>revenue</u> and <u>costs</u> may affect the <u>break-even output</u>.

2) For example, the rate at which revenue changes may decrease if the firm decides to lower its <u>prices</u>. The rate at which <u>costs</u> change may also increase or decrease, e.g. if the <u>cost</u> of <u>supplies</u> changes.

> **BUSINESS EXAMPLE**
>
> The two break-even diagrams below show the effect of Pin-Chit Ltd. <u>lowering</u> its prices from £4 per unit in 2018 to £3.50 per unit in 2019 on the <u>break-even output</u>.
>
>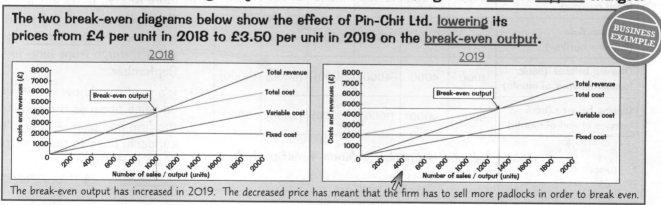
>
> The break-even output has increased in 2019. The decreased price has meant that the firm has to sell more padlocks in order to break even.

The margarine of safety — just use your breakfast analysis...

Q1 A company which makes t-shirts has calculated that its break-even level of output is 1300 units. Its actual sales for one financial year is 2500 units. Calculate the company's margin of safety.

Theme 1: Topic 1.3 — Putting a Business Idea into Practice

Cash Flow

Cash flow — a handy thing for a business to know, and also GCSE Business students as it happens...

Cash *is Not the Same Thing as* Profit

1) Cash is the money a company can spend immediately. A business needs cash in order to pay its employees, its suppliers and overheads (these are ongoing expenses, e.g. rent or lighting).

2) Profit is the amount of money a company earns after costs have been taken into account. So a business can make a profit if it earns more than it spends but still run out of cash if it uses its cash to invest in other assets for the business.

Assets are valuable items owned by the business (e.g. equipment, buildings), or money owed to the business.

3) Cash flow is the flow of all money into and out of the business. When a firm sells its products, money flows in (cash inflow). When it buys materials or pays wages, money flows out (cash outflow).

Net cash flow = cash inflows – cash outflows for a given period of time

4) If a company has positive cash flow then there is more cash inflow than cash outflow for a particular time period. Positive cash flow means that a company has no problem in making payments. However, it may also mean that the company is losing opportunities to invest in ways that might improve it (e.g. in new equipment).

5) Positive cash flow is still not the same thing as profit, though — a company may make a profit if overall it earns more than it spends, but still have poor cash flow (e.g. if cash inflow does not occur in time to make cash outflow requirements).

Cash Flow *Forecasts Help Firms to* Anticipate *Problems*

1) A cash flow forecast lists all the inflows and outflows of cash that appear in the budget (a forecast of all of the firm's likely expenses and revenue).

2) It can be used to show when the firm may face a lack of cash. A lack of cash could lead to the firm failing, because it may be unable to pay its debts (this is called insolvency), unless it sells off its assets.

3) The firm can use the forecast to determine when it will need a short term source of finance to cover its costs.

BUSINESS EXAMPLE

Cash Flow Forecast — Footy Fanzines Ltd.	April	May	June	July	August	Sept
Total receipts (cash inflow)	15 000	12 000	5000	5000	16 000	16 000
Total payments (cash outflow)	12 000	12 000	10 000	10 000	12 000	12 000
Net cash flow (inflow – outflow)	3000	0	(5000)	(5000)	4000	4000
Opening balance (bank balance at start of month)	1000	4000	4000	(1000)	(6000)	(2000)
Closing balance (bank balance at end of month)	4000	4000	(1000)	(6000)	(2000)	2000

closing balance = opening balance + net cash flow

Numbers in brackets are negative.

The opening balance for a month will be the closing balance for the previous month.

Here's an example of a cash flow forecast for a firm publishing football magazines.

1) In June and July, when the football season's over, the net cash flow is negative because more money flows out than in.

2) The firm can see it will need a source of extra finance to get it through from June to September.

3) It's useful to know this in advance because it means the firm can plan — it won't suddenly have to panic in June when it starts to run out of money.

Cash outflow — *it's just money down the drain...*

Cash flow is quite easy once you've understood how the figures are worked out. Make sure you can understand the figures in that table, and that you know why cash flow is super important.

Cash Flow — Credit

A firm's cash flow will <u>change</u> if they give their customers <u>longer to pay</u> for products — this is called <u>credit</u>.

Credit Terms **Can Affect Cash Flow**

<u>Credit terms</u> tell you <u>how long</u> after agreeing to buy a product the customer has to <u>pay</u>.
This can affect the <u>timings</u> of a business's cash flows.

BUSINESS EXAMPLE

1) Stuffin's Turkeys Ltd. sell most of their products in <u>December</u>.

2) This table assumes customers <u>pay when they purchase</u> the product.

Cash Flow Forecast — Stuffin's Turkeys Ltd.						
	October	November	December	January	February	March
Total receipts (cash inflow)	800	1500	12 000	300	500	300
Total payments (cash outflow)	3000	4000	2000	300	200	150
Net cash flow	(2200)	(2500)	10 000	0	300	150
Opening balance (bank balance at start of month)	3000	800	(1700)	8300	8300	8600
Closing balance (bank balance at end of month)	800	(1700)	8300	8300	8600	8750

I'm up for Turkey in December.

3) The table below assumes customers are given <u>two months credit to pay</u>.

4) It's a bit more complicated as the <u>total receipts</u> come in <u>two months after</u> the sale is made.

Cash Flow Forecast — Stuffin's Turkeys Ltd.						
	October	November	December	January	February	March
Total sales this month (for payment in two months)	800	1500	12 000	300	500	300
Total receipts (cash inflow)	200	200	800	1500	12 000	300
Total payments (cash outflow)	3000	4000	2000	300	200	150
Net cash flow	(2800)	(3800)	(1200)	1200	11 800	150
Opening balance (bank balance at start of month)	3000	200	(3600)	(4800)	(3600)	8200
Closing balance (bank balance at end of month)	200	(3600)	(4800)	(3600)	8200	8350

Payment made in 2 months

In February, the total receipts are for the turkeys bought in December. So net cash flow is 12000 − 200 = 11800

5) The main differences are:
- when customers pay immediately there is only <u>one month</u> where extra finance is needed.
- when they pay on <u>two months credit</u> the business will need to arrange extra finance for <u>3 months</u>.

Me, write a naff joke? Give me a little credit please...

Credit makes things a bit trickier, so if you understand the cash flow forecasts on this page you'll be set for whatever forecasts are thrown at you in the exam. Now, just a few questions to get through, then this bit's all done.

Sources of Finance — Small Businesses

You need to know about the different sources of money for firms and some of the pros and cons of each.

Firms Need Finance for Five Reasons

1) New firms need start-up capital (the money or assets needed to set up a business).
2) New firms often have poor initial cash flow — this means that they find it hard to cover their costs (see p.14), so they need additional finance to cover this.
3) Sometimes customers delay payment, so finance is needed to cover this shortfall in (lack of) cash.
4) If a business is struggling, it may need additional finance to meet its day-to-day running costs.
5) Firms may need finance in order to expand — e.g. to buy larger premises.

Small Firms Have Several Sources of Start-up Finance

Short-term sources will lend money for a limited period of time. Examples include:

1) TRADE CREDIT — businesses may give firms one or two months to pay for certain purchases. This is useful for a small firm as they have time to earn the money needed to pay the debt. However, if the firm makes the payment too late, they could end up with a large fee. Paying off the debt will increase the firm's costs, especially if there's a fee, so it will need to make sure that it can cover these costs.

2) OVERDRAFTS — these let the firm take more money out of its bank account than it has paid into it. Overdrafts can allow businesses to make payments on time even if they don't have enough cash. However, they usually have a higher interest rate (see page 36) than other loans and the bank can cancel it at any time. If it isn't paid off, then the bank can take some of the business's assets.

Long-term sources can either be paid back over a longer period of time — usually more than a year, or don't need to be paid back at all. These sources include:

1) LOANS (loan capital) — e.g. bank loans are quick and easy to take out. Like overdrafts, they are repaid with interest and if they aren't repaid, the bank can repossess the firm's assets. However, the interest rate for loans is usually lower than for overdrafts. The business may have to pay the loan back in monthly installments, which will increase their fixed costs. Before taking out the loan, the business should check that they can still break-even (see p.14) with this increase in costs.

2) PERSONAL SAVINGS — A business owner may put some of their own money into the business to get it started or if it is having cash flow problems (see page 16). However, this is risky as the owner could end up losing their money if the business fails.

3) SHARE CAPITAL — Individuals can buy shares in the business. This means that they will have part ownership in the business and the business can use the money gained through issuing shares.

4) VENTURE CAPITAL — This is money raised through selling shares to individuals or businesses who specialise in giving finance to new or expanding small firms. Venture capitalists will usually buy shares in businesses that are risky but have the potential to grow quickly. They will take a stake in the business, and may expect returns more quickly than other shareholders would.

5) RETAINED PROFIT — these are profits that the owners have decided to plough back into the business after they've paid themselves a dividend (see p.29).

6) CROWD FUNDING — This is when a large number of people contribute money towards starting up a business or funding a business idea. It's often used for creative or innovative businesses and usually takes place online. Normally each person only contributes a small amount of money. Sometimes, the people that contribute money may get a reward in return.

Movies have the highest interest rate — everybody's looking at them...

Lots of facts on this page — make sure you can write down every source of finance for a small firm and try to remember one problem with each. Learn, cover the page and start scribbling.

Case Study — Topic 1.3

Now it's time to test all that knowledge that I'm sure you've crammed in there by now... This case study's a bit tricky, so make sure you read everything through a few times (questions and all) before you get started.

Business Report: Putting a Business Idea into Practice

Sashay Handbags

Lizzie owns a business selling handbags, called Sashay Handbags. She started up her business three years ago using her personal savings. In a recent local radio interview to promote the business, Lizzie said that she started the business shortly after having her second child. She also said that she had had a love for handbags from when she was very little.

Lizzie has two employees. Lizzie and her two employees are each paid a salary of £19 000 per year. She also rents a building in which the handbags are made and stored and which has office space. The building costs £1100 a month to rent. On average, each handbag costs £15 to make and market and each sells for an average price of £55. In the third year of the business, Sashay Handbags had sales of 2000 handbags.

Lizzie has recently taken out a loan of £14 000 with her bank in order to fund new equipment and has agreed to pay back £630 of the loan each month. Once the loan is paid off, her repayments will total £15 120.

Case Study Questions

For the following questions, make sure you get all the detail you need from the case study above.
Just leaving out one little detail, e.g. an additional cost that you didn't notice, will affect your answer.

1) Suggest and explain two non-financial aims that Lizzie may have had when starting her business.
2) Explain one disadvantage of Lizzie using her personal savings to finance her business.
3) Suggest and explain one financial aim that Lizzie may have had when starting her business.
4) Calculate the percentage interest on the loan that Lizzie has taken out from her bank.
5) Calculate the yearly fixed costs for Sashay Handbags before taking out the loan, using the details from the case study.
6) Calculate the break-even output in units for Sashay Handbags before taking out the loan.
   State the equation for break-even output in units in your answer.
7) Explain how the break-even output for Sashay Handbags will change once Lizzie has taken out the loan.

If sweet consumption beats no. of pages revised I break even, don't I?...

This should have given you a whizz through some of the main bits of this topic — next up, more questions...

Revision Summary — Topic 1.3

Now you've seen how people can prepare to start up a business and the different types of financial analysis they can use for planning. So, time to get your brain in gear, roll up your sleeves and do some questions.

1) What is meant by the aim of a business?

2) State five financial aims a business might have.

3) State four non-financial aims a business might have.

4) What is meant by a business objective?

5) Suggest how the aims and objectives of businesses in non-competitive and competitive markets might differ.

6) State the equation for calculating a business's revenue.

7) Describe the difference between fixed and variable costs.

8) *Find the total variable costs for a firm if it sells 450 units with a variable cost per unit of £3.

9) Write the equation for calculating the percentage interest a firm has paid on a loan.

10) *A firm's total revenue is £250 000 and its total costs are £100 000.
State whether the firm has made a profit or a loss.

11) What is the break-even level of output?

12) Write the equation for calculating the break-even point for a firm's revenue.

13) *Find the break-even level of output on the break-even diagram below.

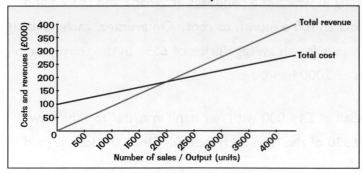

14) What is the margin of safety on a break-even diagram?

15) The rate at which the total revenue of a firm changes with output has increased.
Describe how this will affect the firm's break-even output.

16) What is meant by cash?

17) What is meant by net cash flow?

18) How do you calculate the closing balance for a period on a cash flow forecast?

19) Describe how credit can affect cash flow for a business.

20) Give one disadvantage of using an overdraft compared to other forms of borrowing.

21) Describe what is meant by share capital.

22) Describe what is meant by retained profit.

* Answer to:
q8: 450 × £3 = £1350
q10: The firm has made a profit because its revenue is greater than its costs.
q13: the break-even output is 2000 units.

Theme 1: Topic 1.3 — Putting a Business Idea into Practice

Business Ownership Structures

When an entrepreneur starts a business there are some important decisions to make. For example, what to call the business, what colour the chairs should be and what legal structure the business should have.

Sole Traders — the Easiest Business to Start

Sole trader businesses have just one owner (though the owner may employ other people to work for them). Most small businesses are sole traders. You don't need to do much except start trading. Examples include plumbers, hairdressers, newsagents and fishmongers.

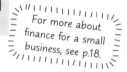

I'm a sole trader

Sole traders — advantages

1) They're easy to set up, which means they're great for start-up businesses.
2) You get to be your own boss.
3) You alone decide what happens to any profit.

Sole traders — disadvantages

1) You might have to work long hours and may not get many holidays.
2) You're unincorporated. This means the business doesn't have its own legal identity. So if anyone sues the business, they'll sue you personally.
3) You have unlimited liability. This means you are liable (legally responsible) for paying back all of the business's debts if it goes bust. As you aren't legally separate from the business, your personal finances are at risk — e.g. you might have to sell everything you own to pay the debts.
4) It can be hard to raise money. Banks see sole traders as risky, so it may be hard to get a loan. You often have to rely on your own savings, or family and friends.

> Some companies have limited liability — which means the amount of debt the owners have to pay back is limited to the amount they invested (see next page).

> For more about finance for a small business, see p.18.

Partnerships are Like Two or More Sole Traders

You get partnerships in businesses like accountancy firms, solicitors and doctors' surgeries. Partnerships generally have between two and twenty partners. Each partner has an equal say in making decisions and an equal share of the profits — unless they have an agreement called a deed of partnership that says different.

Partnerships — advantages

1) More owners means more ideas, and a greater range of skills and expertise — e.g. one partner might be great at sales, while another is good at planning.
2) It also means more people to share the work.
3) More owners means more capital (money) can be put into the business, so it can grow faster.

Partnerships — disadvantages

1) Each partner is legally responsible for what all the other partners do.
2) Like sole traders, most partnerships have unlimited liability (see above).
3) More owners means more disagreements. You're not the only boss. If the partners disagree about which direction the business should go in and how much time to put in, it can get unpleasant.
4) The profits are shared between the partners. So if a sole trader decides to go into partnership with another person, they could end up with less money for themselves.

PRACTICE QUESTION

Wanted: Soul Trader — must have own hood and scythe...

Q1 Jennifer is a sole trader who owns a shoe shop. She is thinking about going into partnership with her brother. Explain one advantage and one disadvantage of Jennifer going into the partnership.

More Business Ownership Structures

Not all start-up businesses are sole traders or partnerships — here are two more structures they could have...

Limited Companies *Are Owned by Shareholders*

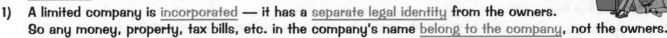

Hmm... there's limited company in this bar

There are two types of limited company — private (see below) and public (p.42).
But both kinds have some important differences compared to sole traders and partnerships:

1) A limited company is incorporated — it has a separate legal identity from the owners.
So any money, property, tax bills, etc. in the company's name belong to the company, not the owners.

2) Being incorporated means the owners have limited liability. If anything goes wrong (e.g. somebody sues the company or it goes bust) it's the company that's liable, not the owners. The owners only risk losing the money that they have invested.

3) It is owned by shareholders. The more shares you own, the more control you get.

Private *Limited Companies — Ownership Is Restricted*

'Private' means that shares can only be sold if all the shareholders agree. The shareholders are often all members of the same family. Private limited companies have Ltd. after their name.

Ltd. — advantages
1) The big advantage over sole traders and partnerships is limited liability — you can't lose more than you invest.
2) It's easier for a Ltd. company to get a loan or mortgage than it is for a sole trader or partnership.

Ltd. — disadvantages
1) They're more expensive to set up than partnerships because of all the legal paperwork.
2) Unlike sole traders or partnerships, the company is legally obliged to publish its accounts every year (although they don't have to be made public).

Franchising *Uses the Brand Name or Product of Another Firm*

1) Some people will start up a business as a franchise of another company.

2) This is where they sell the products or use the trademarks of another firm.
They then give the firm they're franchising from a fee or a percentage of their profits.

3) The product manufacturers are known as franchisors and the firms selling their products are franchisees.

4) Franchises can trade under the name of the franchisee but advertise that they sell a particular manufacturer's products (e.g. car dealerships). Or the franchisee might buy the right to trade under the name of the franchisor. Most of the big firms in the fast-food industry are this type of franchise.

Franchising — advantages
• Customers will already recognise the franchisor's brand so are more likely to buy from the franchisee. This means there's less risk of the business failing.
• As franchises are less risky than starting a business from scratch, it can be easier to get a bank loan to start up.
• The franchisor might provide the franchisee with training, or help with things like management and accounting.

Franchising — disadvantages
• The franchisor might have strict rules about what the business can sell and how it can operate, so the franchisee's freedom is limited.
• The franchisee usually has to pay a lot of money to start the franchise and then make regular payments to the franchisor. These costs may mean they end up with less money than if they started a business from scratch.

Limited lie-ability — you can't help telling the truth...

Private limited companies and franchises are a bit fiddly to get your head round, but you still need to know 'em.

Theme 1: Topic 1.4 — Making the Business Effective

Business Location

Sometimes, success in business is all about being in the right place. When a firm chooses where it's going to locate, there are lots of things to think about to get a site that suits the business and its customers.

Location is Influenced by Different Factors

Suppose a new start-up company Granite King are looking for a location for their new kitchen worktop manufacturing business. They'll want to think about these things...

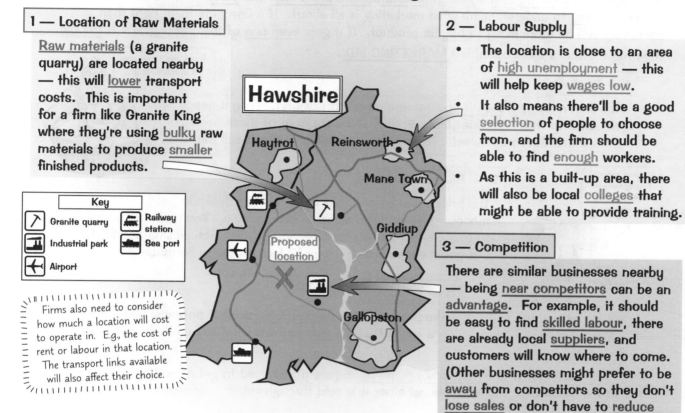

1 — Location of Raw Materials

Raw materials (a granite quarry) are located nearby — this will lower transport costs. This is important for a firm like Granite King where they're using bulky raw materials to produce smaller finished products.

Hawshire

Haytrot Reinsworth

Mane Town

Giddiup

Proposed location

Gallopston

Key
- ↗ Granite quarry
- 🏭 Industrial park
- ✈ Airport
- 🚂 Railway station
- ⛴ Sea port

Firms also need to consider how much a location will cost to operate in. E.g., the cost of rent or labour in that location. The transport links available will also affect their choice.

2 — Labour Supply

- The location is close to an area of high unemployment — this will help keep wages low.
- It also means there'll be a good selection of people to choose from, and the firm should be able to find enough workers.
- As this is a built-up area, there will also be local colleges that might be able to provide training.

3 — Competition

There are similar businesses nearby — being near competitors can be an advantage. For example, it should be easy to find skilled labour, there are already local suppliers, and customers will know where to come. (Other businesses might prefer to be away from competitors so they don't lose sales or don't have to reduce their prices to be more competitive.)

Other businesses might consider these factors:

4 — Location of the Market

- Some firms pay more to transport their finished products than their raw materials. These types of firms find it cheapest to locate near to their customers.
- Some businesses locate near to their market so people know about them and can easily get to them. It also helps them to get sales through passing trade (e.g. from people who walk past the business).

5 — Using the Internet

- The internet means that the location of some firms is more flexible.
- For example, trading over the internet (e-commerce) means manufacturers can locate further from their market, but closer to their raw materials. It may also mean they don't need fixed premises (e.g. a shop) to sell their products from.
- Documents can also be accessed over the internet, which means some businesses no longer need fixed premises for offices. Instead, their employees can work from home and the business can potentially employ people all over the world.

The nature of the business will influence what they prioritise when choosing their location. For example, a business that relies on customers visiting its site is likely to prioritise being close to the market. However, a manufacturing firm may prioritise somewhere close to its raw materials or with a good labour supply.

Location of the market — it's on the High Street, mate...

Make sure you learn the different factors that can influence where a business decides to locate. As a bit of fun, think of a few businesses and decide what location location location factors would be important for them.

The Marketing Mix

Human beings have needs — essential things like water, food and shelter. Once our needs are satisfied, we start to want luxuries too, and we're prepared to pay for them. Marketing is about coming up with a product that people need or want — then making it as easy as possible for them to buy it. Sounds simple enough...

There are Four Ps in Marketing

There are four elements to marketing: product, price, promotion and place — the four Ps. They're the key to understanding what marketing is all about. If a firm gets them right then customers will be more likely to buy its product. If it gets even one of them wrong, it's in trouble. Together the four Ps are called the MARKETING MIX.

But I can't see any Ps in marketing...

1 — Product

The firm must first identify customers' needs (or wants). Then it needs to come up with a product that will fulfil some (or one) of these needs. So spinach flavoured sweets, for example, probably wouldn't sell that well.

Spinach sweets! Finally here to fulfil my every want and need!

2 — Price

The price must be one that the customer thinks is good value for money. This isn't the same as being cheap. You might be prepared to pay a lot of money for a brand new, 50-inch plasma-screen TV, but you'd expect an old basic 12-inch model to be much cheaper.

3 — Promotion

The product must be promoted so that potential customers are aware that it exists and will want to buy it.

4 — Place

Place can refer to the method of distribution (see p.55) used to get a product from the company to the customer. For example, whether it is sold through retailers or sold straight to a customer.

Lots of Factors Can Affect a Business's Marketing Mix

1) The different parts of the marketing mix will affect each other. For example, the quality of the product will affect how much it costs to make, and therefore the price it will be sold for.

2) Changes in technology may affect different parts of the marketing mix. For example, improvements in e-commerce (selling products through the internet) means that more companies are selling their products online rather than in stores. Changes in digital communication have also affected how companies promote their products online (see page 55).

3) What customers need will change over time too. E.g. companies may have to lower their prices for products that use older technology as these products no longer meet the needs of customers.

4) How competitive the market is and what a business's competitors are doing will also affect how a firm balances the elements of its marketing mix. For example, if competitors are offering the same products at lower prices, a business may need to lower its own prices to stay competitive. If a competitor starts selling a brand new product, a business may need to develop its own version of the same product in order to offer a similar range of products to its customers. In a really competitive market, customers may have lots of products to choose from, so businesses may choose to spend more money on promotion to make their products seem more appealing than their competitors'.

I want it all — and I want it now (in the right place at the right price, please)...

Q1 A business which makes cheese is planning to make a new higher quality cheese to satisfy customer demand. Explain how the business is likely to price and promote its new cheese.

Theme 1: Topic 1.4 — Making the Business Effective

The Marketing Mix for Small Businesses

Now you know a little bit about the 'four Ps' it's time to think about how small businesses might handle them.

Small Businesses Need to be Careful With Their Marketing Mix

1) When a business is just starting out, it needs to be very careful to make sure it gets its marketing mix right. This is because it will have fewer sources of finance available to it than more established businesses, so it will be more likely to fail.

2) Here are a few ways in which a small business may focus on each of the four Ps of its marketing mix:

Price

1) Small businesses can't benefit from economies of scale (p.41) in the way that larger businesses can. This is because they won't be able to buy raw materials in large enough quantities and they may not have the right equipment to make their processes as efficient as possible.

2) New businesses also have lots of start up costs, such as buying new machinery.

3) So new and small businesses are likely to have higher prices than large businesses as they will need to cover their costs in order to survive.

Product

1) Small businesses won't have much money to spend on developing lots of different products.

2) This may mean that they will have a smaller range of products compared to larger businesses.

3) They may instead focus on providing higher quality products — e.g. they may choose to make their products using job production rather than flow production (see p.58).

Promotion

1) Methods of promotion such as TV advertising are unlikely to be used by small firms since they're very expensive. A small firm is likely to use cheaper methods, such as flyers or free samples.

2) Promoting the right brand (the overall image of the company) is really important — especially for a new business as it will be trying to establish an image with its customers.

3) Small businesses are more likely to promote to local customers (unless they are mainly based online), which is likely to affect the way in which they promote themselves. E.g. it may be more effective to advertise in local rather than national newspapers.

Place

1) Small businesses are unlikely to produce products in large enough quantities to sell through very large retailers. And large retailers may also not want to sell products from a new, unrecognised brand in case no one wants to buy the products.

2) So many small businesses may choose to sell directly to customers or through smaller retailers.

BUSINESS EXAMPLE

1) Jacob has started a new business selling cards for all occasions.

2) He only has a small amount of start-up finance and so decides to start his business by selling to customers via an e-tailer (see p.55) in order to avoid the costs of renting space.

3) He has a range of 15 different cards, all of which he makes himself. Other online card makers have over 100 different cards, so he decides to make his using much higher quality materials.

4) He pays a small fee to the online e-tailer to have his products promoted on its website.

Podkin Veg Shop's marketing strategy was doomed to failure...

...they only had three peas... Oh dear, you can have some time off for that. I'll sit and think about what I've done...

Business Plans

It's vital that a business has a <u>clear idea</u> of what it's going to do if it wants to be successful — this is where the <u>business plan</u> comes in. You need to know <u>why</u> businesses have them and <u>what</u> they should contain.

The Plan is for the *Owner* and *Financial Backers*

1) A <u>business plan</u> is an outline of <u>what</u> a business will do, and <u>how</u> it aims to do it.

2) Anyone wanting to <u>start a business</u> should have a plan, but they're also useful when an <u>existing firm</u> wants to make <u>changes</u>.

3) A business plan forces the owner to <u>think carefully</u> about what the business is <u>going to do</u>, how it will be <u>organised</u> and what <u>resources</u> it needs. This allows the owner to calculate how much <u>money</u> is needed.

4) The plan can be used to <u>convince financial backers</u> (e.g. banks) that the idea is a <u>sound investment</u>. The business owner can show the financial backer <u>information</u> about how the business will <u>operate</u>, which should help the backer decide how likely it is that they'll get their <u>money back</u>.

5) Writing a business plan should also help to <u>reduce</u> the <u>risks</u> of a new business idea.

6) If the business is a <u>bad idea</u>, the <u>planning</u> should help the owner or the financial backers realise this at an <u>early stage</u> — before they've wasted <u>time and money</u> on an idea that was never going to work.

7) For a new business, the business plan helps managers decide what <u>objectives</u> need to be set to achieve their <u>aims</u> once the business is up and running.

8) They can also help entrepreneurs make <u>business decisions</u>. For example, if they have a <u>sales forecast</u>, they should know how much <u>stock</u> they'll need to buy in order to <u>meet demand</u>.

The Business Plan Describes *How* the Business will be Run

There is no single <u>correct way</u> to write a business plan — but most good 'uns for new businesses include all of the information below:

1) <u>The business idea</u> (p.2) — this should explain <u>what</u> the firm is <u>all about</u>. It could include details of the <u>product</u> the firm will be selling, such as how the firm will achieve its <u>unique selling point (USP)</u> (p.2).

2) <u>Business aims and objectives</u> (p.11-12) — <u>aims</u> usually say something <u>general and obvious</u>, e.g. "To be the market-leading sandwich shop in Kent." <u>Objectives</u> are more <u>specific</u>, e.g. "To average 160 sandwich sales per lunchtime over 4 years."

3) <u>Target market</u> — the plan should explain <u>who</u> the business is aiming to sell to. This should be backed up by <u>market research</u> (p.5-8) showing that the target market will be interested in buying the product.

4) <u>Marketing mix</u> — the plan should describe <u>how</u> the business will sell its products with a <u>marketing mix</u> using the <u>4 Ps</u> (p.24).

5) <u>Location</u> (p.23) — the plan should describe <u>where</u> the business will locate and <u>why</u>. For example, whether it wants to be near its <u>target market</u>, or near its <u>suppliers</u>.

6) <u>Finance</u> — the plan should explain how much <u>money</u> is needed to <u>start up</u> the business, and identify <u>where</u> this money will come from. There should be a <u>cash flow</u> forecast and forecasts of the business's <u>costs</u>, <u>revenue</u> and <u>profits</u>. There should also be <u>ratios</u> to show any backer the <u>likely return</u> on their investment.

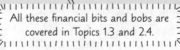

I just need to get a hammer then I'll show you the money.

All these financial bits and bobs are covered in Topics 1.3 and 2.4.

Fear not, Mrs Bank Manager, for I have a cunning plan...

The best laid business plans might not stop a fledgling business from going under — but anyone starting a firm without one would need improbable amounts of luck to survive. In short, plans are important. Learn.

Case Study — Topic 1.4

That's almost it for Making the Business Effective, but you need to make sure you're set up for answering any questions about all this in the exams. So here's a nice case study to help you get to grips with it all...

Business Report: Making the Business Effective

Scoop of the Day

Sophie has decided to set up a business called Scoop of the Day — a café that sells ice cream sundaes. She'll set up the café as a sole trader. Sophie has decided to open the café in the town of Worthbury, but isn't sure exactly where to set it up. She looks at three possible locations for the new café. A summary of her research is shown in the table below:

Location	Cost of rent per month	Description
12 Market Street	£1900	The building is on a busy shopping street. There are two other cafés on the street which sell hot drinks and pastries. The other shops are mainly clothes shops.
Mega Mall	£2500	The pitch is in the food court of a busy shopping centre. The surrounding shops are all food outlets, including a shop selling cookies and another selling frozen yoghurt.
Sutcliff Park	£1650	The building is next to a park popular with families. There are no other cafés in the area. During the summer there is an ice cream van by the park gate.

In order to promote her opening day, Sophie is deciding whether to print some flyers or do a TV advert for a free-to-view channel. Once she has done the research and decided, all of this information will go into her business plan, along with other details about how the business will be run.

Case Study Questions

Time for a few questions to see what you've learnt. Don't worry if you find them tricky to begin with — just go back and have another read through of the topic.

1) Explain one possible reason why Sophie has decided to set up her company as a sole trader.

2) Explain why Sophie should print out flyers to promote her café, rather than do a TV advert.

3) Sophie wants to apply for a bank loan to help fund setting up her business.
   Explain one reason why a bank may agree to give Sophie a loan and one reason why it might not.

4) Recommend which location Sophie should choose for her new café. Give reasons for your answer.

I scream, you scream — that's just case studies, I'm afraid...

Well, there you go. Another case study, all done and dusted. Now time to check the freezer for some ice cream...

Revision Summary — Topic 1.4

Hopefully now you know how businesses choose their legal structure, location and marketing mix to make the business as effective as possible — and then how they bung it all into a business plan. This topic's not easy, so have a flick back if you need to remind yourself about some bits before you answer these questions.

1) What is a sole trader business?

2) True or false? A sole trader is responsible for all the debts of a business.

3) Describe what is meant by a 'partnership'.

4) What is meant by the term 'limited liability'?

5) Describe two disadvantages of private limited companies, compared to sole traders or partnerships.

6) What is franchising?

7) State one advantage and one disadvantage of setting up a franchise compared to starting up a new business.

8) Explain why each of the following factors can affect the location of a business:
   a) the location of the market,
   b) the location of raw materials,
   c) the internet.

9) Give one advantage to a business of locating itself in an area of high unemployment.

10) Give one reason why it may be useful for a business to locate itself near to its competitors.

11) Explain why a high-street retailer and a manufacturing firm may approach choosing the location for their business in different ways.

12) Which 'p' in the marketing mix refers to the way in which a firm sells its products to its customers, e.g. through retailers?

13) Why do businesses use promotion?

14) Describe how e-commerce may affect the marketing mix.

15) Explain how competition may affect how much money a business spends on promotion.

16) Describe what a small business may focus its promotion on in its marketing mix.

17) Explain why a small business might not sell its products through large retailers.

18) Explain how a business plan may help a business to obtain a source of finance.

19) Explain how a business plan may help to reduce risk for an entrepreneur.

20) Give one piece of information that would be included in the business idea on a business plan.

21) Explain why market research needs to be carried out before writing a business plan.

22) State three pieces of financial information that should be included in a business plan.

Stakeholders

A <u>stakeholder</u> is <u>anyone</u> who's affected by a business. Even <u>small businesses</u> may have lots of stakeholders.

Different Stakeholders *Have Different* Ideas of Success

Different stakeholders are affected by the business in <u>different ways</u>. This means they have different <u>opinions</u> about what makes a firm <u>successful</u> and what its <u>objectives</u> should be. For example:

The <u>owners</u> are the most important stakeholders. They make a <u>profit</u> if the business is successful and <u>decide</u> what happens to the business. In a <u>limited company</u>, the <u>shareholders</u> are the owners (see p.22). Shareholders usually want <u>high dividends</u>, and a <u>high share price</u>.

> Dividends are payments that the shareholders get if the company makes a profit. The more shares a shareholder owns, the higher their dividend will be.

<u>Managers</u> and other <u>employees</u> are interested in their <u>job security</u> and <u>promotion prospects</u>. These are improved if the firm is <u>profitable</u> and <u>growing</u>. Employees also want a <u>decent wage</u> and <u>good working conditions</u>. So they may benefit most when objectives are based on <u>profitability</u>, <u>growth</u> and <u>ethics</u>.

A firm buys its raw materials from <u>suppliers</u>. If the firm is profitable and grows they'll need more materials and the supplier will get more business. So suppliers benefit most when the firm sets objectives based on <u>profitability</u> and <u>growth</u>.

The <u>local community</u> where the business is based will suffer if the firm causes <u>noise and pollution</u>. They may gain if the firm provides <u>good jobs</u> and <u>sponsors</u> local activities. If the business <u>employs</u> local people, these employees will then have money to spend in <u>local shops</u>, which is good for the local economy. So the local community may benefit when objectives are based on <u>minimising environmental impacts</u>, <u>ethical considerations</u>, <u>profitability</u> and <u>growth</u>.

The <u>government</u> will receive <u>taxes</u> if the firm makes a <u>profit</u>. They may benefit most when objectives are based on <u>profitability</u>, <u>growth</u>, or <u>job creation</u>.

<u>Customers</u> want <u>high quality</u> products at <u>low prices</u>. They benefit when objectives are based on <u>customer satisfaction</u>.

A <u>pressure group</u> is an organisation that tries to influence <u>what people think</u> about a certain subject. They can influence the <u>decisions</u> a firm makes by creating <u>bad publicity</u> for the firm if they don't agree with the firm's actions. E.g. in 2015, <u>farming pressure groups</u> such as Farmers For Action, held nationwide protests about the <u>low prices</u> some <u>supermarkets</u> paid for <u>milk</u>. Many pressure groups are satisfied when businesses set objectives based on <u>ethical considerations</u> or <u>minimising environmental impacts</u>.

Stakeholders Influence Business Decisions *to Varying Degrees*

1) The <u>owners</u> make the <u>decisions</u> in a firm, so they're the <u>most influential</u> stakeholders.

2) However, they need to consider the interests of <u>other stakeholders</u> when they're setting their objectives.

3) Often, stakeholders will have <u>conflicting opinions</u> about the firm's objectives and its activities.

4) The firm may decide to <u>ignore</u> the opinions of some stakeholders, but they'll need to take others into account if they want to <u>survive</u> as a firm. For example:

- No business can ignore its <u>customers</u>. If it can't sell its products it won't survive.
- A business may want to <u>hold onto its money</u> for as long as possible, but <u>suppliers</u> will become unhappy if they're not paid on time.
- If a business doesn't have happy <u>workers</u> it may become <u>unproductive</u>.
- But a company may not mind being <u>unpopular</u> in the <u>local community</u> if it sells most of its products somewhere else.

I thought you said stay colder.

Stakeholders — vampires are terrified of them...

...but you don't need to be. Just remember that people affected by a business are called stakeholders and they can influence a firm's objectives. That's stakeholder, not steakholder. Unless you want to look like a proper muppet.

Technology and Business

The growth of the internet and the development of computers and other technological thingies have shaken up the business world. You won't get far in business these days without a load of chips and motherboards.

E-Commerce Means Buying and Selling Online

1) E-commerce is using the internet to buy or sell products.

2) Many firms now have websites where customers can buy their products.

3) E-commerce means that firms can reach wider markets compared to just having traditional shops — e.g. a small business in Dorset could end up selling products to someone in New Zealand.

4) E-commerce can be really convenient for consumers — it means they can buy products from all over the world, at any time of the day and they don't have to spend ages queuing up to buy products.

5) Firms have had to adapt to e-commerce as it's become more important. For example, they've had to build websites, employ IT specialists and develop systems to distribute products to online customers.

Firms can Communicate Digitally

Firms regularly need to communicate with their stakeholders (see p.29).
There are many ways firms can use technology to do this:

WEBSITES: Websites are a great way to communicate with customers — e.g. by posting blogs or providing customer service (such as FAQs). Websites can also be used to publish reports to shareholders.

EMAIL: Email is a very quick way of communicating with stakeholders, either on a personal level (e.g. to respond to a customer query) or on a bigger scale (e.g. to tell all employees they can go home early).

MOBILE APPS: These are programs used on mobile devices, such as smartphones or tablets. They are usually used by firms to communicate with customers, for example by giving information about where stores are located, the products the company sells and any special offers.

LIVE CHATS: Live chats are an instant messaging service. They have many uses — e.g. employees can use them to talk to each other from different locations, or customers can use them to speak with a customer service advisor via the internet.

Looks like a great web site you've got there, Ethel.

VIDEO CALLS: Employees who work for the same business in different locations may use video calling to hold meetings, rather than travelling to meet. This can also be a good way for businesses to communicate with important shareholders, who may all live in different places.

Social Media is Becoming More Important to Businesses

1) Social media (see p.6) makes it really easy for users to share information with other users — information can be in many forms, such as written messages or articles, pictures, videos, or links to other sites.

2) This means social media is a great way for businesses to communicate — it can be used to display lots of different types of information, it can be updated regularly and it can be seen by loads of people at once.

3) Businesses use social media for all sorts of purposes — e.g. to provide customer service, to advertise their products, or to promote local events.

An app a day keeps the business doctor away...

Customers expect businesses to be up to date with technology. Nowadays people are used to being able to find information instantly, at any time. Businesses that don't change will probably have a hard time surviving.

More on Technology and Business

Not so long ago, you'd have been laughed at if you said you wanted to <u>pay</u> for your burger using only your <u>eyes</u>. These days it doesn't seem so far-fetched. All this <u>new technology</u> certainly keeps firms <u>on their toes</u>.

Technology Has Made it Easier for Us to Pay for Products

1) There are now lots of different <u>payment systems</u> that can be used to pay for products. For example:

- <u>Online payments</u> — Nearly all firms allow you to pay online by entering your <u>debit or credit card details</u>. But there are other online payment systems (e.g. <u>PayPal</u>) that mean you <u>don't</u> have to enter your card details on <u>every website</u> you buy from, and offer a <u>higher level</u> of <u>cyber-security</u> (so your bank details are less likely to get nicked).
- <u>Chip and PIN</u> — this is where you put your <u>debit or credit card</u> into a terminal (a machine at a checkout) and enter your <u>unique PIN</u> to pay. If you lose your card, you know that someone else can't go on a spending spree with it unless they know your PIN.
- <u>Contactless payments</u> — this is where you pay for something just by holding your <u>debit or credit card</u> or <u>smart device near</u> a terminal. (Using a smart device for contactless payments involves downloading an <u>app</u> first — e.g. Apple Pay™ or Google Pay™ payment service.)

2) Having <u>safer</u> and <u>easier</u> payment systems can <u>encourage</u> customers to <u>shop</u> with the firm.

3) <u>Faster</u> payment methods also mean that businesses can serve <u>more customers</u> in any given time, so their revenue could increase.

Technology has Changed the way Businesses Operate

1) Firms need to <u>adapt</u> to <u>changes in technology</u> so they stay <u>competitive</u>. For example, if a firm's competitors are communicating with customers using <u>apps</u> then the firm should also consider doing this.

2) Businesses can often use new technology to carry out <u>processes</u> in place of people. This can lead to <u>reduced costs</u> in the long term — e.g. because <u>fewer man-hours</u> are needed to carry out tasks.

3) However, adapting to new technology can be <u>very expensive</u>. For example, a business may have to <u>buy equipment</u> or <u>train staff</u> to use new <u>computer systems</u>. They may also need to <u>hire staff</u> with the <u>skills</u> to use the new technology.

4) New technology can lead to <u>increased sales</u> for a business. For example, <u>e-commerce</u> may boost a firm's sales as they can reach a <u>bigger market</u>. Modern <u>payment systems</u> may lead to increased sales as it's <u>easier</u> and <u>faster</u> for people to buy products so they may buy products <u>more often</u> from the firm.

5) New technology can also affect a firm's <u>marketing mix</u> (see p.24). For example, <u>e-commerce</u> means that customers have <u>more choice</u> of firms to buy from as they can buy from firms in <u>places</u> all over the <u>world</u>, not just in their <u>local area</u>. This means that firms may need to change their <u>pricing strategies</u> or the way they <u>promote</u> their products to become <u>more competitive</u>. The growth of <u>social media</u> means that many firms are choosing to <u>promote</u> their products through this channel rather than through more traditional routes, such as newspaper adverts.

BUSINESS EXAMPLE

1) In 2015, Katie Patel bought Glisten Up Cars, a <u>car wash</u> firm. When she bought the firm it was close to going <u>bust</u>, but Katie made it <u>profitable</u> again within two years.

2) Katie bought <u>handheld contactless payment terminals</u>, which meant that people could pay for their car wash from their cars, rather than having to pay in cash or go into the office. This was <u>more convenient</u> for customers, so <u>sales increased</u>.

3) Katie also set up a <u>website</u> to <u>inform</u> customers about the firm, and set up <u>social media accounts</u> to <u>advertise</u> the firm and <u>promote</u> its special offers. These measures also led to <u>increased sales</u>.

If only more things were contactless — like rugby in PE for example...

Keeping up with new technology can really help a firm — making things faster and easier is the name of the game.

Theme 1: Topic 1.5 — Understanding External Influences on Business

Employment and the Law

'Employment law' describes the many different laws associated with the relationship between employers and employees. The laws are generally about pay, recruitment, discrimination and health and safety.

Businesses Have to Pay Staff a Minimum Amount

1) There are laws about the minimum amount employers have to pay their staff.

2) Workers aged 22 and under but of school leaving age have to be paid the National Minimum Wage (NMW) — the exact amount depends on the age of the worker and the type of work. Workers aged 23 and over have to be paid the National Living Wage (NLW) — this is slightly more than the National Minimum Wage.

- The NMW and NLW mean that companies can't cut their costs by paying workers less than the legal minimum. If they do, they're breaking the law.

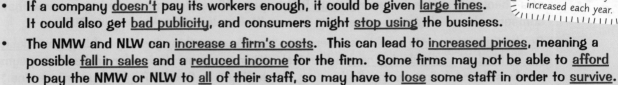 *The NMW and the NLW are usually increased each year.*

- If a company doesn't pay its workers enough, it could be given large fines. It could also get bad publicity, and consumers might stop using the business.

- The NMW and NLW can increase a firm's costs. This can lead to increased prices, meaning a possible fall in sales and a reduced income for the firm. Some firms may not be able to afford to pay the NMW or NLW to all of their staff, so may have to lose some staff in order to survive.

- The NMW and NLW can have benefits for companies though — they can lead to better motivated staff and increased productivity.

There Are Laws About Recruitment

1) Recruitment procedures must not discriminate against anyone because of, for example, their religion, gender, race, age, sexual orientation or because of disabilities. This is covered by the Equality Act 2010.

2) Firms must also make sure that any new recruits have a legal right to work in the UK. This can involve extra work for firms as they may have to carefully check new recruits' documents (e.g. passports and visas), but employing people illegally can result in big fines and possibly even the closure of the firm.

Businesses Can't Discriminate

1) Apart from recruitment (see above), the other main equal opportunities issue covered by the Equality Act 2010 is pay — all employees must be paid the same if they do the same job (or work of equal value) for the same employer.

2) If a company is found to have discriminated against someone, they'll have to pay compensation.

3) If any employee in a company is accused of discrimination, the company could also be held responsible. So companies need to take reasonable steps to prevent discrimination within the workplace — such as staff training and writing company policies about equal rights.

The Workplace Needs to be Safe

1) Health and safety legislation helps to make sure that risks to people at work are properly controlled.

2) Firms need to carry out risk assessments to identify possible dangers and take reasonable steps to reduce the risks. E.g. accident books need to be kept, and first-aiders trained. All staff must receive health and safety training and suitable equipment must be provided — e.g. hard hats on building sites.

3) A safe working environment should mean fewer accidents, and so fewer injuries. And hopefully it means a more productive workforce too — since people should need less time off work to recover.

4) Following health and safety laws can be expensive — e.g. paying for staff to go on safety courses.

5) But businesses that don't follow health and safety laws can be prosecuted, fined and even closed down.

6) They may also have to pay compensation to anyone who's injured, and could get bad publicity.

The law is fragile — careful not to break it...

Making sure all business activities are within the law can take time and be expensive, but all firms need to do it.

Consumer Law

There are laws <u>restricting</u> how firms <u>sell their products</u> — the aim is to <u>protect the consumer</u>. If these laws weren't in place, some businesses might be tempted to be <u>a bit dishonest</u>. Like the time I bought a new TV that turned out to be an egg-whisk. Oh, come on — we've all done it.

The Consumer Rights Act Sets Conditions for Products

The <u>Consumer Rights Act 2015</u> covers how goods and services can be sold. It basically states that goods should meet <u>three criteria</u>:

1 — The product should be fit for its purpose

The product has to <u>do the job</u> it was <u>designed</u> for — if you buy a bucket, say, it's not much use if it leaks water out of the bottom.

2 — The product should match its description

- The way a business describes a product it's selling is called a '<u>trade description</u>'. It's <u>illegal</u> for a retailer to give a <u>false trade description</u>.
- This includes the <u>size</u> or <u>quantity</u> of the product, the <u>materials</u> it's made from, and its <u>properties</u>.
- It's also illegal to claim that a product has been <u>endorsed</u> or <u>approved</u> by a person or an organisation unless it really has been.

...and it's magic and fires lasers and does your maths homework and makes you really attractive...

3 — The product should be of satisfactory quality

- This means that the product should be <u>well made</u> — it shouldn't fall apart after a couple of uses.
- It also means that it shouldn't cause <u>other problems</u> for the buyer — e.g. a <u>fridge</u> should keep food <u>cold</u>, but it shouldn't make a <u>noise</u> like a jet plane at the same time.

If products don't meet the legal requirements, customers can ask for their <u>money back</u>, a <u>repair</u> or a <u>replacement</u>.

Consumer Laws Affect Businesses

1) If a business <u>breaks</u> consumer law it is faced with the <u>cost</u> and <u>inconvenience</u> of having to refund the customer, or repair or replace their item.
2) The case could even end up in <u>court</u> if the customer is <u>unhappy</u> with the business's response about their item (which <u>costs</u> the business <u>even more</u> if the customer wins the case).
3) As well as being expensive, breaking consumer law can <u>harm the reputation</u> of the business, which could lead to a <u>reduction in sales</u>.
4) So businesses have to be <u>very careful</u> when selling products and services to their customers.
5) They need to make sure they <u>train their staff</u> properly, so they sell products <u>accurately</u> and understand what a <u>customer's rights are</u> if they are unhappy with a product.

Firms need to make sure they keep <u>up to date</u> with <u>all legislation</u> that they need to follow — any <u>changes</u> to the legislation could mean that they need to <u>make changes</u> to their business. For example, a change to <u>consumer law</u> could mean that they have to <u>rewrite</u> any <u>terms and conditions</u> they give their customers and <u>retrain</u> their staff.

Consume a law — I'm told it tastes like chocolate...

Q1 Martine buys a new pencil case from a company's website. The product description online says it's suitable for standard stationery needs, and should arrive within three days of purchase. When the pencil case arrives, Martine discovers it is too short to fit a normal sized pen. Explain one way in which the company selling the pencil case has broken consumer law.

Unemployment and Government Taxes

The economic climate can have a huge effect on firms, but it's something that they can't control. The economic climate includes many different economic conditions — first up, unemployment and taxes.

Unemployment is a Big Problem

People are unemployed when they're able to work but can't find a job. The level of employment (the number of people in work) changes over time, and this can have a big effect on businesses.

1) Unemployment means the economy as a whole produces less output than if everyone was employed. So everyone suffers from unemployment — in theory at least. UK unemployment was very high in 2010 — around 2.5 million. In 2016, this had fallen to about 1.6 million.

2) Some firms can actually benefit from unemployment. They may be able to pay lower wages if there are lots of unemployed people desperate for a job. It can also mean they can fill jobs easily. In areas of high unemployment, the government may even give grants to firms who open and provide jobs in the area. These factors may encourage a firm to grow when unemployment is high.

3) But there can also be big problems for businesses when there are high levels of unemployment. Less employment means lots of people have less disposable income. This can lead to a lack of demand for products, so sales can fall. A firm may respond by, e.g. reducing prices, reducing output or making staff redundant.

Disposable income is the money that people have left once they have paid tax.

4) It may also be a problem if firms hire people who have been unemployed for a while — people may lose skills while they're unemployed, so firms may need to retrain them.

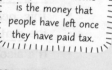

1) DV Murray is a small construction firm in the UK. The recession in 2008 meant that the firm had to make many of its construction workers redundant.

2) In 2014, the growth of the economy meant that DV Murray took on many new contracts and needed to recruit more workers.

3) Many of the workers it recruited had not worked in the construction industry since 2008, so DV Murray had to spend time and money on retraining these staff.

Tax is Money That Goes to the Government

1) Both consumers and businesses have to pay tax. For example, consumers have to pay tax on money they earn (called income tax). Businesses have to pay tax on their profits. They also have to pay other taxes, such as environmental tax on activities that harm the environment, and tax on premises they own.

2) Tax rates are set by the government. Changes to tax rates can have a big impact on businesses:

- If the amount of income tax that consumers need to pay falls, they will have more disposable income. This means that consumer spending is likely to increase, leading to increased revenue for firms. The opposite is true if income tax increases — consumer spending is likely to fall.

- If the amount of tax that a business needs to pay increases, it reduces the amount of money they have available to reinvest. This can lead to slow growth for a business. If environmental tax increases, a firm may try to be more environmentally-friendly to avoid paying extra tax, e.g. by recycling more. But the tax increases may force the firm to find ways to cut costs in order to survive or meet their profit targets, e.g. by making staff redundant. They may also consider relocating the business abroad to a country where businesses pay less tax.

- If the government reduces taxes that a business has to pay, it means the business will have more money available to reinvest. This can help businesses to grow. However, lower business taxes might encourage firms from abroad to set up in the UK. This increases competition in the market and may lead to a fall in sales for UK businesses if they don't compete well.

Having disposable income is no excuse for throwing your money away...

Make sure you know the ins and outs of unemployment and tax and the effects they can have on businesses.

Inflation and Consumer Income

Another two economic conditions now and it's two which are always changing — prices and incomes.

Inflation is an Increase in the Price of Goods and Services

In general, the price of goods and services inflates (goes up) over time. The prices of hundreds of products that an average UK household would buy is regularly tracked. The percentage increase in the price of these products over time is used to measure the rate of inflation. Inflation can have many different effects on a business. For example:

- **CONSUMER SPENDING**: When inflation rises, consumer spending is likely to go up in the short-term — people rush to buy more products before prices go up even more. This creates extra revenue for a business, which can lead to higher profits (depending on how much the increase in inflation has affected its costs). However, if wages don't go up at the same rate as inflation, demand for products can start to fall (there's more about this below).
- **COST OF LABOUR**: With high inflation, employees can put pressure on employers to increase wages so that they can afford the higher prices being charged for the things they need. This can increase a business's costs and reduce its profits.
- **GLOBAL COMPETITION**: A high inflation rate makes UK exports (products sold to other counties) expensive, so UK firms become less competitive globally. This means that a firm that sells lots of exports may see its sales fall. However, when inflation is low, sales of exports are likely to increase.

When inflation is high, business growth tends to be low. Businesses find it hard to predict what is going to happen to their costs and sales. This can make them reluctant to take risks and invest in their business.

Changes in Income can Affect Businesses

Over time, the amount that people earn (their income) increases. However, incomes don't necessarily change at the same rate as inflation.

Income rises at a slower rate than inflation...

- People will have to spend a greater proportion of their income on things they really need — such as food.
- So they'll have less money left to spend on luxuries, such as going to the cinema, or buying new shoes — the demand for these products will go down.
- This means businesses that provide luxuries will suffer — their sales are likely to go down, leading to lower profits. They could lower their prices or spend more on advertising to increase demand again, but this is still likely to lead to lower profits.
- However, some businesses will benefit if people's incomes are relatively low. Stores selling goods at discount prices are likely to see sales go up as more customers will be making an effort to buy things as cheaply as they can.

If inflation is rising at a faster rate than income, income is said to be going down in 'real terms'.

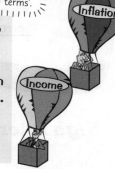

Income rises at a faster rate than inflation...

- People will be spending a smaller proportion of their income on things they need. This means they'll have more money to spend on luxuries, and the demand for these goods and services will go up.
- Businesses providing luxuries will see an increase in sales and their profits are likely to increase.
- Stores selling goods at discount prices may see their sales and profit go down as people start worrying less about getting things for the cheapest possible price.

PRACTICE QUESTION

Protect yourself from falling prices — wear a hard hat...

Q1 George owns a fine dining restaurant. Explain how his sales might be affected if:
  a) Income is rising at a faster rate than inflation.
  b) Inflation is rising at a faster rate than income.

Interest Rates

On to another <u>economic condition</u> now — <u>interest rates</u>. Many <u>businesses</u> and <u>consumers</u> will <u>borrow</u> money at some point. The amount of money they have to pay back depends on the <u>interest rate</u>.

Interest is Added to Loans and Savings

No, Meera, I said it was about <u>borrowing</u>.

1) As you read on p.13, when you <u>borrow</u> money, you usually have to pay it back with <u>interest</u> — this means that you pay back <u>more</u> than you borrowed.

2) If you <u>save</u> money, you <u>earn</u> interest — the amount of money in your savings account will <u>increase</u> over time.

- The amount of interest you pay or earn depends on the <u>interest rate</u> — it's usually given as a percentage. The <u>higher</u> the interest rate, the <u>more</u> you pay or earn.

- In the UK, the <u>Bank of England</u> sets the <u>base rate</u> of interest — most other interest rates are linked to this. The base rate <u>fluctuates</u> (goes up and down) depending on how good the <u>economy</u> is.

Low Interest Rates Lead to Increased Spending

1) When the interest rate is <u>cut</u>, it's <u>cheaper</u> to <u>borrow</u> money. But you get <u>less interest</u> when you <u>save</u> money at a bank.

2) When rates are <u>low</u>, firms and consumers <u>borrow more</u> and <u>save less</u>.

3) Consumers have <u>more money</u> to spend, so <u>demand</u> for goods and services <u>goes up</u>. This means that firms are likely to make <u>more profit</u> and may need to <u>increase output</u>.

4) Firms that borrow money to finance their spending (e.g. by using <u>overdrafts</u> and <u>loans</u>) will have <u>smaller</u> interest repayments, so they have more money available to spend on <u>other parts</u> of the business. They may also choose to <u>borrow more</u> while interest rates are low, e.g. if they want to grow the business.

High Interest Rates Lead to Decreased Spending

1) <u>Increases</u> in interest rates have the <u>opposite</u> effect to cuts — <u>borrowing</u> money becomes more <u>expensive</u>, but <u>savers</u> get <u>better returns</u> on their investments.

2) Firms and consumers will have <u>less</u> money available to spend — they'll be paying higher rates on money they've borrowed. They're also likely to be trying to <u>save more</u>, in order to take advantage of <u>higher returns</u>.

3) This <u>reduces demand</u> for products, so firms often <u>sell less</u> and their <u>profits</u> may <u>go down</u>.

4) It may also mean that firms can't <u>afford</u> to <u>pay</u> everyone who works for them — so some people may be made <u>redundant</u>, and <u>unemployment</u> may go up.

As revision increases, my interest rate goes down...

Interest rates can be tricky to get your head round. They're like a seesaw — if interest rates go down, spending goes up. If interest rates go up, spending goes down. Have another read to make sure you know why this happens.

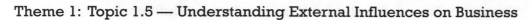

Exchange Rates

Exchange rates are the final economic condition you need to know about — hurrah. Exchange rates tell you how currencies compare. They're really important for firms that buy from or sell to other countries.

Exchange Rates Convert between Currencies

1) If a company wants to import products, they'll have to pay for the product in the currency of the country it was made in. For example, if a British firm is importing goods from the US, they'll have to pay for them in dollars, rather than pounds.

2) An exchange rate is the price at which one currency can be traded for another.

3) Exchange rates are affected by the economy of the country that uses the currency, and by the global economy. This means they can change over time.

> Importing means buying goods from another country. Exporting means selling goods to another country.

- In June 2016, the UK voted to leave the European Union.
- This created a lot of uncertainty about what would happen to the UK economy.
- As a result, the value of the pound dropped overnight.
- The day before the result was announced, £1 was worth $1.48. After the result was announced, £1 was worth just $1.36.

A Weak Pound is Good for Exporters, Bad for Importers

1) If the value of the pound decreases, you'll be able to buy fewer dollars (or other currency) for the same price as before.

2) Pounds are cheaper, so British exports become less expensive abroad — resulting in more sales and higher profits for British firms that export products to other countries.

3) The weak pound also makes it more expensive for foreign firms to sell their products in the UK. That's good news for British firms that compete with goods imported from abroad — they won't have to reduce their prices so much to stay competitive.

4) But it's bad news for British firms that use imported raw materials — these are now more expensive so the production costs of these firms are higher. They'll need to increase the price they sell their products for to cover their costs, which could cause their sales and profits to go down.

5) The result is that the UK will have more exports and fewer imports.

- If £1 = $1.50, a British cricket ball that costs £5 will sell in the US for 5 × 1.50 = $7.50. And a baseball that cost $6 in the US can be sold for 6 ÷ 1.50 = £4 in the UK.
- If the value of the pound falls so that £1 = $1.30 the £5 cricket ball would sell in the US for 5 × 1.30 = $6.50. The $6 baseball can now be sold in the UK for 6 ÷ 1.30 = £4.62.

> You don't need to be able to do these calculations — but make sure you understand how changing the exchange rate can affect the cost of importing or exporting.

A Strong Pound is Bad for Exporters, Good for Importers

1) An increase in the value of the pound makes exports more expensive and imports cheaper. It's just the opposite effect to the example above.

2) British firms that export products to other countries are likely to see their sales and profits go down — their products will be more expensive so fewer people will buy them. They may decide to move part of their business abroad so they can trade in the currency of the country where they sell their products, meaning they will be less affected by the exchange rate.

3) British firms that import raw materials will be able to make products more cheaply, so their profits may go up.

---

1 sultana = 0.84 raisins on the currant exchange...

This is a difficult page, so check you really understand it all. A weak pound means it's expensive to buy things from abroad, and cheap for people from abroad to buy things from us. A strong pound means the opposite.

Case Study — Topic 1.5

There's a lot to learn about external influences on business and a lot of it is pretty tricky.
Try to block out any of your own external influences now as you concentrate on this case study.

Business Report: Understanding External Influences on Business

Frame the Wall Ltd.

Frame the Wall Ltd. is a photo printing firm. The business started in 1999 as a small shop on the high street. However, after several years they found that their sales started to fall. This prompted them into setting up an e-commerce website. The website successfully increased their sales, which resulted in them recruiting five new staff members by 2007.

For the next three years the firm's profits continued to grow. At the start of 2010 the owners had discussions about the future plans for the business. They researched how some experts predicted the economic climate would change in the coming years. Their findings are shown in the table below.

	Predicted Change 2010-2013
Tax paid on profits	A significant fall
Inflation rate	A fall from its current high level
Consumer income	A rise at a faster rate than inflation
Interest rates	A slight rise from the current low level

After careful consideration, Frame the Wall Ltd. planned to reinvest a large percentage of their profit in order to grow the business in the next three years.

Case Study Questions

All that information wasn't just so you can ace a general knowledge quiz.
You'll need to use it to answer the following questions.

1) Suggest why the development of Frame the Wall Ltd.'s website led to increased sales.

2) Outline two areas of employment law that Frame the Wall Ltd. would have taken into account during the recruitment procedures for their new staff.

3) Discuss the likely opinions of the following stakeholders on Frame the Wall Ltd.'s decision to reinvest a large percentage of the profit:
a) employees, b) shareholders.

4) Using the information in the table, analyse Frame the Wall Ltd.'s decision to concentrate on growing the business in the three years after 2010.

It's going to be a photo finish to the end of the topic...

Case studies may not be the most fun thing in the world but it's important to practise answering questions like these before the exams. Remember — you already have the knowledge. The key is to apply it to a new situation.

Revision Summary — Topic 1.5

Business owners have to stay aware of all the influences covered in this topic if they want their business to have a chance of surviving. And for your exams, you need to know about them too. So have a go at these questions to test how much you remember.

1) Describe what is meant by the term 'stakeholder'.
2) Describe how a pressure group may influence a firm's activities.
3) Other than pressure groups, state four possible stakeholders in a business.
4) Explain why a firm's costs may increase if it starts using e-commerce.
5) Other than social media, state three ways a business can communicate digitally with its stakeholders.
6) Explain why social media is a good method of communication for businesses.
7) Give three different payment systems that can be used by businesses.
8) Explain why setting up faster payment systems can be beneficial for a business.
9) Explain how using new technology may have a positive impact on a business's costs.
10) Explain one way in which new technology might change a firm's marketing mix.
11) Explain how the law has some control over what a business pays its workers.
12) How might a business be affected if it discriminates against its workers?
13) True or false? Businesses are legally obliged to provide employees with necessary safety equipment.
14) State two possible consequences to a business of failing to follow health and safety laws.
15) State three criteria that goods should meet in order to follow consumer law.
16) Explain why breaking consumer law can be expensive for a business.
17) Explain why some firms may benefit from high levels of unemployment.
18) State two negative impacts that high levels of unemployment can have on a business.
19) Give one type of tax a business has to pay.
20) Explain how a business might be affected if the amount of tax consumers have to pay increases.
21) What does 'inflation' mean?
22) Explain why consumer spending might increase if inflation increases.
23) Describe a type of business that could suffer if inflation is rising at a faster rate than incomes.
24) Explain what happens to consumer spending when interest rates fall.
25) Explain how a firm with lots of loans will be affected by rising interest rates.
26) What is an exchange rate?
27) Explain why a weak pound can benefit British companies that export goods.
28) Explain why a strong pound can benefit a British business that imports goods.

Business Growth

There are loads of big businesses out there — but all of them have had to grow at some point.
You need to know about both internal and external growth...

Internal Growth is Low Risk but can be Slow

1) Internal growth (or organic growth) is when a business grows by expanding its own activities.

2) Internal growth is good as it's relatively inexpensive. Also, it generally means the firm expands by doing more of what it's already good at — making its existing products. So it's less likely to go wrong.

3) The firm grows slowly, so it's easier to make sure quality doesn't suffer and new staff are trained well.

4) But because internal growth is slow, it won't be right for a business that wants to grow quickly.

5) Here are two methods of organic growth:

1 — Targeting new markets

*   This is when a business aims to sell its products to people who it hasn't tried to sell to before.
*   Firms can use new technology to target new markets. E.g. they could use e-commerce (p.30) so people can buy products even if they don't live near a store. Technology may also mean items are cheaper to produce, so a firm might be able to lower its prices and target a lower income market.
*   A firm could also set up branches in other countries so they can sell directly in markets abroad.
*   They could also change the marketing mix (p.24) of the product (e.g. the price or the way its promoted) so that it appeals to a new market.

2 — Developing new products

*   Selling a brand new product will increase sales for a business, allowing it to grow.
*   To sell a new product, firms need innovation — this is when someone comes up with a new product or way of doing things. Often, innovation comes about as a result of research and development.

External Growth is Faster but More Risky

1) External growth (inorganic growth) usually involves a merger or takeover.

2) A merger is when two firms join together to form a new (but larger) firm.

3) A takeover is when an existing firm expands by buying more than half the shares in another firm.

4) There are four basic ways a firm can merge with or take over other firms.

*   Join with a supplier — This allows a firm to control the supply, cost and quality of its raw materials.
*   Join with a competitor — This gives the firm a bigger market share, so it will be a stronger competitor.
*   Join with a customer — This gives the firm greater access to customers and more control over the price at which its products are sold to the end-user.
*   Join with an unrelated firm — This means the firm will expand by diversifying into new markets. This reduces the risks that come from relying on just a few products.

Ey up, it's another student-lamppost merger.

5) Less than half of all takeovers and mergers are successful. It's very hard to make two different businesses work as one. Management styles often differ between firms — the employees of one firm may be used to one company culture and not be motivated by the style used in the other.

6) Mergers and takeovers can create bad feeling, especially if the firm didn't agree to being taken over.

7) Mergers and takeovers often lead to cost-cutting. For example, there's no point a business having two head offices — the business will have lower fixed costs if it just has one. This cost cutting may mean making lots of people redundant, so it can lead to tension and uncertainty among workers.

Toenails — masters of internal growth...

Growth can be hard work, but it can actually allow a firm to reduce its prices. See the next page for more...

More on Business Growth

You saw on the last page how companies might choose to <u>grow</u> or <u>expand</u>. Now it's time to expand your knowledge further and get to grips with one of the <u>main benefits</u> of being a big firm — lower average costs.

Larger Firms Benefit from Economies of Scale

1) When a firm expands, its <u>output</u> (the amount of products it makes) will <u>increase</u>.

2) Its <u>costs</u> will also increase. For example, <u>variable</u> costs will increase as the firm has to buy more <u>raw materials</u> and <u>fixed costs</u> might increase if the firm has <u>more buildings</u> or <u>staff</u>.

3) Often, however, <u>costs</u> will increase at a <u>slower rate</u> than output.

4) This means that the <u>average cost</u> of making <u>one product</u> (the average unit cost) is <u>cheaper</u> once the firm has expanded.

> *See page 13 for more on variable and fixed costs.*

5) These reductions in <u>average unit cost</u> are called <u>economies of scale</u>.

6) Economies of scale can happen for <u>different reasons</u>. Here are <u>three</u> of them:

- Larger firms need <u>more supplies</u> than smaller firms, so will <u>buy supplies in bulk</u>. This normally means they can get them at a <u>cheaper unit price</u> than a small firm.

- Larger firms can afford to <u>buy</u> and <u>operate</u> more <u>advanced machinery</u> than smaller firms which may make processes <u>faster</u> or <u>cheaper</u> to run (e.g. they might not need so many <u>staff</u>).

- The law of <u>increased dimensions</u> means that, for example, a factory that's <u>ten times as big</u> will be <u>less than</u> ten times as <u>expensive</u>.

7) As the <u>average unit cost</u> of making each product is <u>lower</u>, firms can make <u>more profit</u> on each item they sell.

8) Also, lower average unit costs mean larger firms can afford to <u>charge</u> their customers <u>less</u> for products than smaller firms can. This may make customers <u>more likely</u> to <u>buy</u> their products, leading to <u>increased sales</u> and <u>more profit</u>.

> Geoffrey, with regret, you're fired.
>
> Freida! I said expand the business!

9) The profits can be <u>reinvested</u> into the business so it can <u>expand even more</u>.

There are also Diseconomies of Scale

It's not all good news for large firms though — growth brings with it the risks of <u>diseconomies of scale</u>. These are areas where growth can lead to <u>increases</u> in <u>average unit costs</u>. For example:

1) The <u>bigger</u> the firm, the <u>harder</u> and <u>more expensive</u> it is to <u>manage</u> it properly.

2) Bigger firms have <u>more people</u>, so it can be harder to <u>communicate</u> within the company. Decisions <u>take time</u> to reach the whole workforce, and workers at the bottom of the organisational structure feel <u>insignificant</u>. Workers can get <u>demotivated</u>, which may cause <u>productivity</u> to go down.

> *See pages 70-71 for more on organisational structures.*

3) The <u>production process</u> may become <u>more complex</u> and more difficult to <u>coordinate</u>. For example, <u>different departments</u> may end up working on very <u>similar</u> projects without knowing.

PRACTICE QUESTION

Economies of scale — don't diss them...

Q1 Lucky Dice are a company that make board games. They have recently expanded by building an extension to double the size of their factory and by hiring ten more staff members.
a) Explain how the factory extension could affect the average cost of producing each board game.
b) Explain why the business expansion might mean Lucky Dice charge less for their games.
c) Explain one way that the business expansion might cause problems for Lucky Dice.

Sources of Finance — Large Businesses

You saw on page 18 how small firms can raise money. Well larger firms (those that are established or growing) need to raise money too and here are a few ways that they can do it...

Large Businesses *can Use Funds from Internal Sources...*

Retained Profits

These are profits that the owners have decided to plough back into the business after they've paid themselves a dividend (see p.29). But larger companies (e.g. PLCs — see below) are under pressure from shareholders to give large dividends, reducing the profit they can retain.

Fixed Assets

Firms can raise cash by selling fixed assets (assets that a business keeps long-term, e.g. machinery/buildings) that are no longer in use. There's a limit to how many assets you can sell, though — sell too many and you can't go on trading.

...or External Sources

Loan Capital

1) You saw on page 18 that small businesses can take out loans. They then pay the money back over a fixed period of time with interest.

2) Banks need security for a loan, usually in the form of assets such as property. If things go wrong, these assets can be sold to pay back the loan. Large firms can normally take out larger loans than small firms, as they usually have more valuable assets.

3) Also, established firms may find it easier to get loans than new firms because they can prove to the bank that they've been profitable over a longer period of time. This means banks will see them as less risky.

Share Capital

1) If a business becomes a limited company (see p.22 and below) it can be financed using share capital — money raised by selling shares in the business.

2) Finance from share capital doesn't need to be repaid (unlike a loan).

3) However, selling shares means that the original owner(s) will get a smaller share of the business's profits and lose some control over how the business is run.

Public Limited Companies *Can Sell Shares on a Stock Market*

You saw on pages 21-22 the types of structure that a small business might have. As a business grows, the owners might decide to make it a public limited company (a PLC). 'Public' means that shares in the company are traded on a stock market, and can be bought and sold by anyone. This can bring a lot of extra finance into the business, especially if the shares are in high demand, as this will increase their value. There are advantages and disadvantages to becoming a PLC:

Selling shares on the stock market is known as 'stock market floatation'.

PLC — advantages

1) Much more capital can be raised by a PLC than by any other kind of business.

2) That helps the company to expand and diversify.

3) PLCs are incorporated and have limited liability (p.22), so if things go wrong, the owners only lose the amount of money they've invested.

PLC — disadvantages

1) It can be hard to get lots of shareholders to agree on how the business is run. Each shareholder has very little say (unless they own a lot of shares).

2) Someone could buy enough shares to take over the company — if they can convince shareholders to sell.

3) The accounts have to be made public — so everyone (including competitors) can see if a business is struggling.

4) PLCs can have hundreds or even thousands of shareholders, so there are lots of people wanting a share of the profits.

Roll up, roll up! Get your soups on the stock market...

Money might not grow on trees, but larger firms have more options than smaller ones when it comes to finance.

Theme 2: Topic 2.1 — Growing the Business

Changes in Business Aims and Objectives

On pages 11-12 you saw how aims and objectives are used to run a business. Well, these aims and objectives aren't set in stone. As the business and the world around it changes so can the aims and objectives.

A Company's Aims and Objectives Can Change in Different Ways

As a business evolves, its aims and objectives are likely to change. For example, it might want to...

Change whether it aims to survive or grow

A new, start-up business's aims are likely to be focused on survival. However, once it is stable, aims might be centred around growth and maximising profits for reinvestment. But if the economy takes a downturn, the business might start struggling, and its aims could once more become focused on survival.

Change the size of its workforce

For example, if a business is expanding, it might aim to recruit more staff. If a business has recently taken over another firm, it might aim to reduce the size of its workforce so it doesn't have multiple people carrying out the same role.

Enter or exit new markets

A business could aim to enter a new market, e.g. by targeting a different group of people in the same place, or by starting to sell products in a new location. This could be because the business is growing, but may also be because their existing markets are shrinking and they need to find new places to sell their items. If a product isn't selling well in a particular market, the business's aims are likely to change so that they exit that market.

Change the size of its product range

For example, if a business has a product that's selling really well, it might aim to bring out more products in the same range with different features. If it has products in a range that don't sell well, it might aim to decrease the product range and concentrate on promoting and growing its best-selling products.

Aims and Objectives May Change for External or Internal Reasons

Firms also need to change their aims and objectives to keep up with the dynamic (ever-changing) business environment. For example:

- New legislation — companies may need to adjust their aims and objectives when new laws are introduced. E.g. in 2016, a new living wage was introduced. This affected many companies' profit aims and objectives, as they had to pay higher wages.
- Changes in market conditions — if a market grows, a company may alter its aims to focus on growing sales. However, if a market shrinks, a company might be more focused on survival or targeting new markets. If a market gets more competitive, a company might focus more on maintaining its market share or maximising sales, rather than maximising profits or growing its market share.
- Changes in technology — companies need to keep up to date with new technology, especially if their competitors are using it. They may need to alter their aims and objectives so they spend more money on getting new equipment and training staff rather than investing in growth.

Factors within the company can also affect its aims and objectives. For example:

- Performance — if a company performs better or worse than expected, aims and objectives may be changed. For example, if it sells more than expected one month, future sales objectives might be increased to match this.
- Internal changes — changes within the company can affect what its aims and objectives are. For example, if the management changes, then the new managers might have different priorities for the business, which will cause its aims and objectives to be changed.

I would have got the bullseye, but my aim was changed...

Make sure you know how a business's aims and objectives might change over time and the different factors that can affect them — from the government shaking up the laws, to shiny new managers with shiny new ideas for a firm.

Globalisation

Better technology makes it easier to communicate and travel round the world. Which causes globalisation...

Globalisation Means the World is More Interconnected

1) Globalisation is the process by which businesses and countries around the world become more connected. It means that it has become easier and more common for businesses to import products (buy them from abroad), and export products (sell products to other countries).

2) The effects of globalisation can have many different impacts on businesses:

- IMPORTS — firms have a larger market to buy from, so they may be able to buy supplies more cheaply, which reduces costs and can increase profits. However, more imports means there's more competition in a country. Firms may be forced to reduce their prices to stay competitive.
- EXPORTS — being able to export goods easily means firms have a larger market to sell to. This can lead to increased sales and higher profits.
- BUSINESS LOCATION — globalisation has made it easier for businesses to locate parts of their business abroad (e.g. to set up stores, factories or offices overseas). This may allow them to reduce their costs so they can make more profit, e.g. if they start producing goods closer to where they get their raw materials from, their transport costs will fall. Some firms may also set up in countries where labour is cheaper, which helps to keep their costs down.
- MULTINATIONALS — single businesses operating in more than one country are known as multinationals. When a big, multinational business enters a new country, firms already in that country may need to change the way they operate in order to compete successfully.

Firms Face Barriers to International Trade

Firms can't just buy and sell products across the world willy nilly — governments have set up tariffs and trade blocs as a way of trying to control international trade:

- Tariffs — these are taxes on goods that are being imported or exported. They make products imported into a country more expensive than those that are produced domestically (in the home country). This helps domestic firms stay competitive.
- Trade blocs — these are groups of countries that have few or no trade barriers between them, e.g. they can trade with each other without having to pay tariffs. Firms from countries outside the trade bloc will find it hard to compete with those inside, as their prices will be affected by having to pay tariffs.

Firms Need to be Able to Compete Internationally

Having a global market means there can be lots more competition. So businesses need to be able to stand out from the competition. Here are a couple of ways they do that:

- Firms can use e-commerce to sell products via the internet. This means they can compete overseas without having to set up stores and infrastructure in foreign countries, which keeps their costs down.
- Firms may change their marketing mix in different countries. E.g. they can change prices to make sure they're competitive, or target products and promotion at the country's culture.

1) McDonalds is a multinational company. Stores in different countries have slightly different menus to appeal to the customers in those countries.

2) E.g. in India, none of their products contain beef, as many Indians are Hindu, so don't eat beef. In China, they have a special, seasonal menu to fit in with Chinese New Year.

BUSINESS EXAMPLE

It's a small world after all...

Q1 Pillow Perfect is a shop that makes and sells pillow cases in the UK. It wants to expand internationally. Describe two things Pillow Perfect could do to compete internationally.

Ethical Considerations

There are lots of things a business can do to make sure it's being <u>fair</u> and <u>honest</u>. Many <u>stakeholders</u> are concerned about how businesses <u>behave</u> towards others, and whether they act in an <u>ethical</u> way.

Ethical Issues Have Become Important for Businesses

1) Ethics are the <u>moral principles</u> of right and wrong.

2) Many firms have their own <u>ethical policies</u>. This means they've developed ways of working that <u>stakeholders</u> think are <u>fair</u> and <u>honest</u>.

3) The ways that UK firms treat <u>employees</u> and <u>suppliers</u> in <u>other countries</u> raises many ethical issues.

> - In some countries, it's not illegal for people to work <u>very long hours</u> for very <u>low pay</u>. Some firms set up <u>factories</u> in these countries to reduce their <u>labour costs</u> — many people think this is <u>unethical</u> if it <u>exploits workers</u> from foreign countries.
> - Businesses can write <u>codes of conduct</u> for any <u>factories</u> they have overseas. This helps to ensure that the workers are treated <u>ethically</u>. For example, they can put <u>limits</u> on the <u>number of hours</u> somebody can work each week so they don't get <u>too tired</u>. They could carry out <u>checks</u> to make sure the code is being <u>followed</u>.
> - Firms that buy <u>raw materials</u> from <u>developing countries</u> can choose to buy from <u>Fair Trade sources</u> — this means people in developing countries who produce the goods (e.g. cocoa farmers) are paid a <u>fair price</u> so they can earn decent wages.

4) Businesses need to treat their employees <u>in the UK</u> ethically too. E.g. businesses should <u>reward</u> staff <u>fairly</u>, keep <u>personal details</u> about staff <u>private</u> and provide a <u>comfortable working environment</u>.

5) <u>Treating people well</u> isn't the only ethical issue for a business. For example, when <u>promoting</u> products, firms have to follow <u>codes of practice</u> — they can't be <u>dishonest</u> or <u>insult other brands</u> in adverts (although competing products can now be compared in a fair way). Some products can't be advertised <u>at all</u> — e.g. cigarette adverts are banned on health grounds.

6) Firms are also under pressure to carry out <u>product development</u> in an ethical way — this means using <u>non-toxic</u> materials, paying close attention to <u>safety</u>, and not using <u>animal testing</u>.

Acting Ethically can have Benefits and Drawbacks

1) There can be a <u>trade-off</u> between <u>behaving ethically</u> and making the most <u>profit</u> for a firm.

2) Ethical policies can be <u>costly</u>. For example, by treating workers fairly and making sure they are all paid a fair wage, a business is likely to have <u>higher labour costs</u> than if they didn't work ethically.

3) Also, if a firm is committed to using <u>ethically sourced materials</u> (e.g. fair trade products) they may find it <u>more difficult</u> to <u>find suppliers</u> and have to pay a <u>higher price</u> for their <u>materials</u>.

4) These increased costs mean that a firm doesn't make as much <u>profit</u> on each item that it sells. It could put its <u>prices up</u> so that it makes more profit per item, but higher prices might lead to <u>lower sales</u> (so the business still ends up with <u>less profit</u>).

5) However, despite potentially making less profit, many firms are <u>still keen</u> to work ethically.

6) Firms might change their <u>marketing</u> to emphasise the fact that they have strong ethical policies. For example, the Co-op advertises all its chocolate as from <u>Fair Trade</u> sources. By advertising its ethical policies, a business might <u>gain customers</u> and <u>increase its profits</u> — there are plenty of people who think that ethical practices are <u>more important</u> than price.

7) Acting ethically can have a positive effect on <u>other stakeholders</u> as well. For example, some <u>shareholders</u> will be more likely to invest in a firm if it has shown that it behaves <u>ethically</u>. Treating <u>staff</u> ethically can mean workers are <u>more motivated</u>, which should make the firm <u>more productive</u>.

No animals were harmed in the making of this page...

...but several writers were prodded with forks. Not really — CGP is an ethical business. Ethical policies can reduce profits, but there's also plenty of demand for ethical goods — so there's always a trade off for businesses.

Environmental Influences

Being a "green" business involves more than just buying a pot of green paint and a paintbrush...

Businesses Can Reduce Their Impact on the Environment

1) All businesses can have an impact on the environment. For example, by producing waste that ends up in landfills. Factories, cars and lorries can also cause air, noise and water pollution.

2) People are worried that the combined impact of global businesses is damaging the Earth at the moment. For example, many firms use resources that are non-renewable (e.g. coal and oil) — if these resources run out there's no way we can replace them. Also, many business activities release carbon dioxide and other gases into the atmosphere — these are thought to be contributing to global warming.

3) Many businesses are now aiming to be more sustainable — this means working in ways that won't damage the Earth for future generations. Here are some ways they might do that:

- Use less packaging and recycle more so that less waste goes to landfills.
- Dispose of hazardous waste carefully so that it doesn't pollute land or water.
- Use more efficient machinery that is less polluting to the air, or quieter machinery that causes less noise pollution.
- Use more renewable energy resources (e.g. wind or solar power), and electrical goods that are more energy efficient.

There are Pros and Cons to Being Environmentally Friendly

1) As people become more aware of environmental issues, consumers are changing their buying decisions — people are now buying more "environmentally friendly" products.

2) Taking environmental issues seriously can give firms a competitive advantage — a "green image" can attract new customers and increase sales.

3) However, there can be a trade-off for a business between being sustainable and making profit. For example, buying new equipment and developing new processes in order to be more sustainable can be expensive. Firms have to weigh up the benefits against the negative effect it could have on their profits.

A Business Might Change its Policies due to Pressure Groups

1) Pressure groups are organisations that try to influence decisions made by the government or by businesses (see p.29).

2) If a pressure group runs a campaign against a certain firm or industry (e.g. by highlighting areas where it could be more environmentally friendly or ethical) customers might start to view the firm or industry in a bad light. This means the firms involved could lose custom if people stop buying from them.

3) To improve their image in the public eye, businesses can change their marketing mix. For example, a business might have to change its products in response to activity from pressure groups — e.g. by making sure the materials are more ethically sourced, or have less of an impact on the environment. It might also run promotional campaigns to repair the negative publicity the pressure group has caused.

- Supermarkets have been under pressure from groups such as WRAP and Friends of the Earth to reduce the amount of food that they waste.
- As customers have become more environmentally conscious, this pressure has increased.
- Many supermarkets have now changed their policies to reduce food waste — e.g. by changing processes with suppliers so food is fresher when it reaches the store, so it's less likely to go off.
- Supermarkets are also changing the products they sell — for example, some sell vegetables that are slightly strange looking for a cheaper price, so farmers don't have to throw them away.

BUSINESS EXAMPLE

Be friendly to the environment — go on, give it a smile...

Businesses can't afford to ignore environmental issues — firms that do may find themselves losing customers.

Case Study — Topic 2.1

Well, if a business grows at the rate of my little sister, then it'll be a multinational in no time... Now test all your new-found knowledge on business growth, etc by doing the questions on this tasty case study.

Business Report: Growing the Business

innocent drinks

innocent drinks is a UK company that was founded in 1998. Its main product is fruit smoothies. **Figure 1**, on the right, shows some of the events in the timeline of innocent drinks. Since 2009, Coca-Cola® has had shares in the company. Coca-Cola® is a multinational soft drinks manufacturer.

innocent drinks is a company that takes being sustainable very seriously. It has several ways in which it is working to make itself more sustainable, including making sure each area of the business meets sustainability standards set by external organisations and reducing energy wasted along its supply chain. It also puts emphasis on ethical policies, such as giving 10% of its profits to charities, including the innocent foundation. The innocent foundation gives money to other charities that are working to help the world's hunger problems.

— 1998 — innocent drinks founded

— 2003 — innocent drinks opens offices in Paris and Amsterdam

— 2007 — innocent drinks expands into Germany and Austria

— 2009 — Coca-Cola® buy 18% shares in innocent drinks

— 2010 — Coca-Cola® buy 38% more shares in innocent drinks

— 2013 — Coca-Cola® buy over 34% more shares in innocent drinks

— innocent drinks launches noodle pots, kids' fruity water and extra juicy smoothies

Figure 1

Case Study Questions

When you have a detailed figure with a case study, like the one above, make sure you read it as thoroughly as the text. You'll then make sure you have all the information you need to answer questions like these...

1) In what year did Coca-Cola® obtain enough shares to take over innocent drinks? Explain your answer.
2) Suggest one benefit to innocent drinks of raising money through share capital.
3) Explain one advantage to innocent drinks of being a multinational.
4) Outline two different internal growth methods innocent drinks have used.
5) What is meant by a company being 'sustainable'?
6) Analyse the possible impacts to innocent drinks of its sustainability and ethical practices.

Innocent... until I own up to taking that last chocolate biccie...

Luckily you can quench your thirst for some more practice questions simply by turning the page...

Revision Summary — Topic 2.1

Well, there we go. One more topic down on your path to Business glory. Now that you've grown your business knowledge, it's time to test yourself with a few questions about Growing the Business.

1) What is organic growth?
2) Explain how a business can use new markets to expand.
3) Explain how innovation can help a business to expand.
4) Describe the difference between takeovers and mergers.
5) Explain two disadvantages of external growth.
6) What are economies of scale?
7) Explain how a company can use fixed assets to raise finance.
8) Give two examples of external sources of finance that may be available to an established business.
9) Explain why becoming a public limited company allows a firm to raise lots of money.
10) Give one disadvantage to a business of becoming a public limited company.
11) Give three examples of how a business's aims and objectives might change as it grows.
12) Explain how an increase in the competitiveness of a market may affect a business's aims and objectives.
13) Explain why changes in technology could affect a business's aims and objectives.
14) Give two factors within a company that may affect the company's aims and objectives.
15) What is globalisation?
16) Explain two ways in which a business might benefit from globalisation.
17) What name is given to a single business operating in more than one country?
18) Explain two ways a business may face barriers to international trade.
19) Give one way in which a business may need to change its marketing mix when it starts selling its products in a different country.
20) Describe three ways in which a firm could make sure it is working ethically.
21) Give one way in which working ethically may improve a firm's productivity.
22) Explain why working ethically might reduce a firm's profits.
23) State two ways in which a business can reduce its impact on the environment.
24) Explain how the profits of a business might be affected if it changes its activities to become more sustainable.
25) Explain one way in which a business might change its marketing mix in response to pressure groups.

The Marketing Mix and The Design Mix

It's back to the four Ps of the marketing mix — they're important for established businesses as well as small businesses. Oh, and a bit of the design mix is thrown in for good measure too.

The Different Parts of the Marketing Mix Affect Each Other

1) You may remember from p.24 that there are four different elements of marketing — product (a good or a service), price, promotion and place. These different elements make up the marketing mix.

2) A business can use the different elements of the marketing mix to make decisions about the business.

3) By having the right combination of the four different elements, a business can have an advantage over its competitors (called a competitive advantage), by attracting and selling to more customers.

4) However, the different elements of the marketing mix can affect each other — this may mean that a business will have to make a compromise between the different elements. For example, a business may have to charge a high price for high quality products.

5) The method of distribution of a product will also affect its pricing and promotion. Products sold online are likely to be cheaper than those sold in stores since the business may have lower fixed costs (e.g. rent). High-street retailers are likely to use displays in their store fronts to attract customers, whereas businesses that sell products online may use more online advertising.

6) The quality and price of the product will also affect how it is promoted — if a product is of low quality but it is quite cheap, then price may be emphasised in promotional material. However, if the product is of higher quality or is more expensive, then the promotional material may emphasise its quality.

Differentiation Can Attract Customers

Differentiation is about making your products or services distinctive in the market — e.g. by changing elements of the marketing mix. These differences should make customers want to buy your product instead of competing products.

A company may not be able to differentiate itself for long — competitors may copy the idea which removes their competitive advantage.

1) Without differentiation, customers will think your product is identical to others.

2) One way to differentiate a product is to give it a unique selling point (USP) — see p.2. This could be a special feature or a service provided by the company, such as fast delivery.

3) You can promote your product in a way that makes it seem different, even if it's not.

4) You can also change the price of the product. Cheaper usually means more appealing to a mass market, but it also means less profit per unit sold. Having a really expensive product can actually make it appear much more luxurious than competitors' products and more appealing to a niche (small and specialised) market.

5) Product design is hugely important for product differentiation. The DESIGN MIX has three main ingredients:

Function — the design must be fit for its purpose. A car without an engine would be a non-starter. Unique features can also help — a razor with seven blades shaves better than a razor with one. Probably.

Cost — a good design will lead to low manufacturing costs. This means higher profits.

Aesthetics (appearance) — a good product should look attractive and distinctive. Packaging can also help a product to stand out (and protect it till it reaches the customer).

USP — Underwater Serving Plates — for the unique dinner party

Q1 A business that specialises in dog food products decides to create a new cat food product. Describe how the business should consider the elements of the design mix when making the new product.

Product Life Cycles

Even firms with great products will find that they don't sell well <u>forever</u> — all products have a <u>life cycle</u>.

*Demand **for a Product** Changes Over Time*

All products go through the same <u>life cycle</u> — but the sales life of some products is <u>longer</u> than others. For example, the sales life of most <u>cars</u> is about <u>ten years</u>, but the sales life of many <u>computer games</u> is only a <u>few months</u>. Whatever the product, its <u>marketing mix</u> will need to <u>change</u> during its life cycle.

1) <u>RESEARCH AND DEVELOPMENT (R&D)</u> is the first stage of a product's life cycle.
   It is used to develop an idea and turn it into a marketable <u>product</u>.

   - <u>Scientific research</u> is often vital for product development. A lot of scientific research is done in universities. It's often "<u>pure</u>" science — without any kind of <u>commercial aim</u>.
   - Large businesses often then have teams of "<u>applied</u>" scientists, who try to use recent scientific discoveries to develop <u>new</u> or <u>improved</u> products to sell.
   - One aim during product development is to find the most <u>cost-effective materials</u> and <u>methods</u> to use.

2) <u>INTRODUCTION</u> comes next — the product is <u>launched</u> and put <u>on sale</u> for the first time. This is usually backed up with lots of <u>advertising</u> and <u>sales promotions</u>. <u>Place</u> is also an important P here — there's no point launching a product in places where nobody will be interested in buying it.

3) <u>GROWTH</u> — During this phase, demand <u>increases</u>, until the product becomes <u>established</u>.

4) <u>MATURITY</u> — Demand reaches its <u>peak</u> during this stage. Promotion becomes <u>less important</u> — businesses will continue to <u>advertise</u> the product, but less than at its launch. As the product's popularity <u>grows</u>, businesses will try to make the product more <u>widely available</u>. Towards the end of this phase, the market becomes <u>saturated</u> and there's <u>no more room</u> to expand.

   > As demand for a product increases, sales of the product will also increase, and vice versa.

5) <u>DECLINE</u> — Eventually demand starts to <u>fall</u> as rival products <u>take over</u>.
   The life cycle is linked to the <u>cash flow</u> of the business during the life of the product.

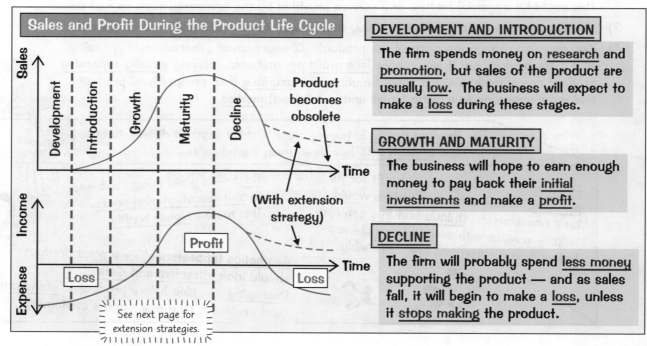

Sales and Profit During the Product Life Cycle

DEVELOPMENT AND INTRODUCTION

The firm spends money on <u>research</u> and <u>promotion</u>, but sales of the product are usually <u>low</u>. The business will expect to make a <u>loss</u> during these stages.

GROWTH AND MATURITY

The business will hope to earn enough money to pay back their <u>initial investments</u> and make a <u>profit</u>.

DECLINE

The firm will probably spend <u>less money</u> supporting the product — and as sales fall, it will begin to make a <u>loss</u>, unless it <u>stops making</u> the product.

Marketing a product? Sounds more like parenting...

So, make a product that people want. Love it and nurture it throughout its life cycle. Then watch as it gets old, becomes unpopular and starts losing you money — products can be so ungrateful. Try not to cry.

Extension Strategies

Over time the sales of products may eventually <u>decline</u>, as you saw on the previous page. But that's not the end of the story — oh no. There are lots of things that businesses can do to <u>keep their products selling</u>. These are called <u>extension strategies</u> — they drag out the life of a product to the bitter end...

Firms May Try to *Extend the Life* of Products in *Decline*

1) Although the sales of all products will eventually decline, firms can take action to <u>extend their life</u>.

Scalpel... needles... sale sign. Come on people, let's move — there's a life to extend here.

2) They might decide to use an <u>extension strategy</u> during the decline phase of the life cycle.

3) If the extension strategy works, the product will make profit for <u>longer</u>.

4) However, it means <u>spending more</u> money on the product — this <u>takes away</u> cash from other parts of the business.

5) Firms have to strike a <u>balance</u> between investing money in supporting <u>old</u> products and in designing <u>new</u> ones.

There are *Several Types* of Extension Strategy

There are <u>lots</u> of ways that firms can extend the life of their products, for example:

1) <u>Adding more or different features</u> — adding new features may increase <u>demand</u> for the product by making it <u>more useful</u> or <u>more appealing</u> to customers.

2) <u>Using new packaging</u> — creating a new packaging <u>design</u> for the product may make it more <u>eye-catching</u>, so that customers are more likely to <u>see</u> it and <u>choose</u> it over competitors' products. A new image for the product may also attract a <u>new target market</u>...

3) <u>Targeting new markets</u> — businesses can find new markets for their products, for example a different <u>age group</u> or <u>country</u>. They can then target their <u>promotional material</u> at the new markets to <u>extend</u> the life of the product.

4) <u>Changing advertisements</u> — by running a new <u>advertising campaign</u>, businesses may be able to make <u>more</u> people aware of the product, or promote it in a way that makes it <u>more appealing</u> to the original market or to a <u>new</u> market.

5) <u>Lowering price</u> — businesses can <u>reduce</u> the price of the product, or use <u>special offers</u> or <u>competitions</u>.

1) Several of these extension strategies are <u>related</u> to each other. For example, changing the <u>packaging</u> of the product may help to <u>target</u> a new market. Businesses may use a <u>combination</u> of several strategies.

2) However, certain strategies may be more <u>beneficial</u> to a business or a certain situation than others.

3) You need to be able to <u>evaluate</u> how useful different strategies will be for a business, or <u>suggest</u> strategies that a business could use.

BUSINESS EXAMPLE

1) Bubbletime is a company that sells <u>shower gels</u> and <u>shampoos</u>.
2) One of its <u>shower gels</u> for <u>babies</u> entered the <u>decline phase</u> of its life cycle.
3) Therefore the company decided to <u>rebrand</u> the product as a shower gel for <u>people with sensitive skin</u>.
4) It designed <u>new packaging</u> and also changed <u>TV adverts</u> and <u>posters</u> for the shower gel, so that they were <u>targeted</u> towards <u>all ages</u> with <u>sensitive skin</u>.
5) This meant that the company was able to <u>extend</u> the life of the product.

Extension Strategies — for when your homework's late...

So, instead of letting them retire gracefully, firms just keep those products working. Some people have no respect.

Price

Time for another of those P's now and it's the one that customers usually think is most important — price.

Businesses Need to Think About Demand When Setting Prices

1) Most businesses aim to make a profit — this means that the money they get from selling their products has to be more than the business's costs.

The total cost of making a product includes the cost of getting it to market too — e.g. marketing and distribution costs.

2) The easiest way to do this is to make the price of each product higher than the total cost of making it.

3) However, firms need to think about how the price of a product will affect demand (the quantity of a product that customers are able and willing to buy). As prices rise, demand for a product tends to fall. So firms need to make sure that the price of a product isn't so high that they won't sell many.

4) Sometimes, a firm may need to set the price of a product lower than the total cost of making it so that there is still a decent level of demand for the product (see next page). In this case the firm may have to rely on making lots of profit on other products in its portfolio so that it doesn't go bust.

Internal and External Factors Influence Pricing Decisions

1) There are many factors to consider when deciding on the price of a product. Some of these factors are internal (controlled by the business) and some are external (not controlled by the business).

Internal

- Technology — The technology used by the business in every step of its process of making and marketing the product will affect pricing. For example, if expensive machinery is needed to make the product, then this may increase the price that it needs to be sold at in order to make a profit. However, in the long-term, machinery may help to reduce costs since, e.g. processes may be more efficient or fewer employees may be needed (see p.59).

- Method of production (see pages 58-59) — Flow production may require expensive machinery but it will also be more likely to benefit from economies of scale compared to job production so products may be cheaper.

Flow production involves making lots of identical products on an assembly line. Job production is when individual products are made one at a time.

- Product life cycle — Where a product is in its life cycle will affect its price. For example, when the product is in the introduction and growth phases a firm may charge a very low or very high price to encourage people to buy it (see next page). When it's in the maturity phase, a firm may need to bring its price in line with competitors' prices (see below). When it's in the decline phase, the firm may need to reduce the price in order to increase demand for the product again.

External

- Competition — If the product is sold in a competitive market, the firm needs to look at what competitors are charging for similar products. If a firm puts its prices too high, customers will just choose a competitor's product. If it puts its prices too low, customers will query whether the quality is as good as its competitors'.

- Market segments — The nature of the market segment that a product is being targeted at will affect its price. For example, if the product is aimed at a segment with a high income, its price will be higher than a similar product aimed at a segment with a lower income.

- Cost of raw materials — This will affect the cost of each unit (individual product). High quality raw materials will lead to high unit costs and so high prices will be needed to cover these costs.

2) A business's pricing decisions are likely to change as it grows. E.g. once it has developed loyal customers and a good reputation, it might be able to increase prices without demand falling too much.

3) On the other hand, as a business grows it can benefit from economies of scale (see page 41). This means that the average cost of making each product falls, so the business can afford to lower prices.

You can't put a price on happiness...

...but you can make examiners happy by knowing the different factors that affect a business's prices.

Pricing Strategies

This is where bosses narrow their eyes and stroke their chins — they need to choose the best <u>pricing strategy</u>.

Here are *Five Pricing Strategies Businesses Can Use*

1) Price Penetration

1) This is where a firm charges a very <u>low</u> price when a product is <u>new</u> to get lots of people to <u>try it</u>.
2) It's a good way to establish a <u>market share</u> for a product in a <u>competitive market</u>.
3) The product will make <u>very little profit</u> at first but once it has become <u>established</u> the firm <u>increases</u> the price. Loyal customers should <u>continue</u> to buy the product despite the price increase.

2) Loss Leader Pricing

1) This is when the price of a product is set <u>below cost</u>. The firm doesn't make a profit on it, but the idea is that customers will <u>buy other products as well</u> (which it does make a profit on).
2) E.g. <u>games consoles</u> are often priced <u>below cost</u> but firms make <u>profit</u> on <u>games</u> that go with them.

3) Price Skimming

It may sound steep, but this is cutting-edge technology.

1) This is where firms charge a <u>high price</u> to begin with — they can usually do this when they know there will be a <u>high demand</u> for the product (e.g. goods that use <u>new technology</u> and have a desirable <u>USP</u>, such as smart TVs).
2) It often works for <u>established firms</u> as they'll have <u>loyal customers</u> who will be <u>willing to pay</u>.
3) The high price helps the firm to <u>increase revenue</u> and to cover any <u>research and development</u> costs.
4) Having a high price also helps to make the product more <u>desirable</u> to people with <u>high incomes</u>, or to a more <u>niche market</u> (e.g. professionals). This can help to improve the firm's <u>image</u> and <u>status</u>.
5) Once the product's <u>established</u>, the firm <u>lowers the price</u> to help it become a <u>mass-market</u> product.

4) Competitive Pricing

1) This is where the firm has to charge <u>similar</u> prices to <u>other firms</u>.
2) It happens most when there is <u>lots of choice</u> and not much product differentiation — e.g. petrol.
3) The firm may make <u>very little profit</u> and have to find ways <u>other than price</u> to <u>attract</u> customers.

5) Cost-Plus Pricing

Firms may use this method if they're <u>not</u> in <u>price competition</u> with other producers. The firm works out the <u>total cost</u> of making the product, and then adds on a certain amount depending on how much <u>profit</u> they want to make while still having reasonable <u>demand</u>. There are <u>two main ways</u> it can be done:

Using a Mark-Up

Work out how much the product costs and then add a <u>percentage mark-up</u>. So if the product costs <u>£2</u> to make, and you want a 25% mark-up, you'd sell it for £2 + 25% = £2.50.

Using a Profit Margin

Work out how much the product costs and increase it to get the <u>profit margin</u> you want. So if the product costs <u>£2</u> to make, and you want a <u>20% profit margin</u>, this means that £2 is 80% of your required selling price. So 80% = 200p, 1% = 200 ÷ 80 = 2.5p, 100% = 2.5p × 100 = 250p. So you'd sell it for <u>£2.50</u>.

Note: mark-up is expressed as a % of <u>cost</u>. Profit margin is expressed as a % of the <u>selling price</u>.

PRACTICE QUESTION

Price skimming — getting 99p to hop across a pond's surface...

Q1 A supermarket sells its own-brand steak pies for less than it costs to make them.
Name the type of pricing strategy the supermarket is using and suggest why it uses this strategy.

Methods of Promotion

Promotion is basically when firms big-up a product so that customers notice it and want to buy it.

Good Branding is Important

1) A firm's brand image is the impression that customers have of the firm or products sold by the firm — e.g. the firm may have a reputation for high quality, luxury products. There may also be a recognisable logo that customers associate with the company or products.

2) Products with a strong brand image are easily recognised and liked by customers. A strong brand image is usually built up over a number of years. It's important that a firm's products, prices, methods of promotion, and the places they sell in all build the right brand image.

3) A firm may create different brand images for different products to target different market segments. E.g. a skincare company may market some products to women and others to men.

4) Developing a brand image and promoting products is expensive for a business, but both should increase the revenue of a firm — through first time purchases and repeat purchases. The business will have planned for this increase in revenue to cover the costs of promotion and branding.

Firms Promote Their Products by Advertising

One way that businesses can establish a good brand image is through effective advertising. Advertising is any message that a firm pays for which promotes the firm or its products. Methods of advertising include:

1) Newspapers — local ones can reach a market segment in a specific geographical area and national ones can reach a wide audience. They're printed often so they're a good way to promote temporary offers. However, the print quality is usually poor and the number of people reading newspapers is declining.

2) Magazines are often aimed at a particular market segment, e.g. people in the same age group or people with similar hobbies. Businesses can use adverts in these magazines to target these specific market segments. Magazine adverts can be pricier than newspaper adverts, but they're better quality and people tend to hang on to magazines for longer.

3) Posters and billboards can be placed near a target audience, stay in place for a long time and be seen daily by lots of people. But people might not look at them for long, so messages need to be short.

4) Leaflets, flyers and business cards are cheap to produce and distribute. They can be targeted at certain areas (which is useful for targeting a market segment in a particular location) and people can keep them until they need the information. But many people see them as 'junk' and throw them away quickly.

5) Television adverts can be seen by a wide audience and include sounds and moving images. They can deliver long messages and help to emphasise the firm's image. On the downside, they're very expensive.

6) Internet adverts can be seen at any time by a large, targeted audience, can include sounds and moving images, and customers can visit the firm's website immediately after viewing the advert. However, there are so many adverts online, people may stop looking at them properly or choose to block them.

Businesses Can Sponsor Organisations and Events

Firms sometimes give money to organisations and events — e.g. schools, TV production firms and exhibitions. In return, their name is displayed by the organisation or at the event. This is called sponsorship. E.g.:

- SPORT — A large firm might stamp its brand name all over an international competition. A smaller firm might only be able to afford to sponsor the local Sunday League team, but the aim is the same.
- TELEVISION — Some soap operas and weather reports are sponsored by well-known brands.

Sponsorship can create a high profile for your business or brand name, it's also a good way to target a market segment that is characterised by lifestyle (e.g. hobbies). But if the thing you're sponsoring starts to get bad publicity, your company's image might suffer too.

I LOVE getting people to move about — yep, I'm totally pro-motion...

Different types of promotion are suitable for different market segments — more on that on the next page...

Methods of Promotion and Place

There are so many ways to promote a business, there's another page with loads of stuff on it, just for you. There's even some info on the final 'p' of the marketing mix — place. I'm sure you're delighted...

Sales Promotion is a Short-Term Method Used to Boost Sales

1) Here are two examples of types of sales promotion:

   - Special offers — businesses may offer a discount on the product for a limited period of time, or two products for the price of one.
   - Product trials — e.g. cafés may offer free samples of new food or drink to get customers interested and to persuade them to buy the new products in the future.

2) An advantage of sales promotion is that it should encourage new customers to try a product. This will boost sales in the short term but could also increase sales in the long term if customers like the product and continue to buy it once the promotion has ended.

3) A disadvantage of sales promotion is that customers get used to seeing products on promotion and may be reluctant to buy them at other times. Also, using regular sales promotions might not be suitable for certain market segments. E.g. it might make a product in a luxury market seem like less of a luxury item, so it won't be useful for targeting a higher income segment that are looking for luxury.

Firms Can Also Use New Technology for Promotion

1) Technology provides many opportunities for promotion. E.g. firms can create social media accounts which advertise their products and improve their brand image. They are also able to make separate accounts for different parts of the business, and so may be able to target specific market segments.

2) An individual's internet search history can be used to create targeted advertising. Web pages have spaces for adverts, but the adverts found in these spaces will depend on what an individual has searched for in the past. So the adverts will be more likely to be something that the individual is interested in, and therefore will be more effective. Technology can also track an individual's location for use in targeted advertising. Although some individuals dislike this, and may be put off the brand.

3) Viral advertising is when adverts are shared on social media and are viewed many (perhaps millions) of times in a short time period. This is good for targeting segments of a market that use social media frequently (e.g. younger age groups).

4) As well as social media and targeted advertising, individuals may also decide to be a part of a business's mailing list. This means that they will get e-newsletters from the business about promotions and offers.

The Place Where Products Are Sold Must be Suitable

1) To make sure that a business's products are available to consumers in the right place the business needs to choose the most appropriate method of distribution. This depends on things like where the consumer is likely to shop, how many consumers they want their products to reach, how quickly they want the product to get to the consumer, and how much customer service the consumer will need.

2) Methods of distribution can include retailers (these sell products to consumers, e.g. from a shop) and e-tailers (these are companies that sell products online — i.e. that use e-commerce).

3) High-street retailers are likely to have employees on hand who customers can talk to, which is less likely for e-tailers, so selling products via retailers may mean that better customer service is provided.

4) E-tailers have many advantages. For example, they can sell to a global market — this means that they will have many more potential customers than if they used stores. They will also have lower fixed costs than retailers, since they won't have to pay to have stores open. This may mean that they can charge less for products.

A sturdy pair of rocket boots — another way to boost sales...

In our modern internety world, more and more firms are cutting out the middlemen and selling directly to consumers.

Theme 2: Topic 2.2 — Making Marketing Decisions

Case Study — Topic 2.2

There's no denying it — there's a lot to learn in this topic. See how well you can apply what you've learned about the world of marketing by reading this real-life case study and answering the questions.

Business Report: Making Marketing Decisions

Nestlé®

Nestlé® is a multinational food and drink manufacturing company. It makes many different breakfast cereals using flow production and sells them directly to large retailers. However, sales of breakfast cereals are falling in the UK. The cereal market is also very competitive, with many other companies and hundreds of cereal products on the market.

Nestlé® produce Shreddies, which are one of the firm's most popular brands of cereal. Since 2007, scenes of older ladies appearing to knit Shreddies have been used in television adverts as well as on other promotional material for Shreddies. Nestlé® created an official 'Knitting Nanas' Facebook® page. On the page they encouraged people to post pictures and videos to find a new Knitting Nana. This was hugely popular and the page obtained over 250 000 fans.

In 2016, Nestlé® launched Shreddies Max, a granola based cereal. Unlike most of the other cereals on the market, Shreddies Max is labelled as being a good source of protein.

Case Study Questions

Now you've read the case study, get your best marketing hat on and have a go at the following questions.

1) Describe how the cereal market is likely to affect Nestlé®'s pricing strategies for its cereals.

2) Explain why Nestle may have decided to launch an advertising campaign for Shreddies.

3) Explain whether the decision to promote Shreddies using the 'Knitting Nanas' television adverts was appropriate for the business and analyse the impact the campaign is likely to have had on sales.

4) Explain the impact to Nestlé® of differentiating Shreddies Max.

5) Explain how the demand for Shreddies Max may have changed in 2016-17.

Where does Santa eat his Shreddies? In Nestlé®...

Ho ho ho — that one's a cracker. Answering these case study questions takes a lot of writing and I know you'll be tempted to skip them — but you're bound to get asked about a case study in the exam, so it's all good practice.

Revision Summary — Topic 2.2

Had enough of marketing yet? Of course not — that's why there are even more questions here for you to answer on all of the stuff you've covered in this topic. I'm sure you're delighted...

1) Describe how the quality of a product may affect how it is priced and how it is promoted.

2) What is meant by differentiation?

3) What is the first stage in a product life cycle?

4) Explain how the marketing mix for a product will be different when it's in the introduction stage of its life cycle compared to when it's in the maturity stage.

5) Sketch a graph to show how sales of a product are likely to change throughout its life cycle.

6) What is the purpose of an extension strategy?

7) Give five different types of extension strategy.

8) Explain how a firm's costs will influence the price it charges for a product.

9) Describe how the price of a product may affect demand for it.

10) Give three internal factors that will influence a firm's pricing decisions.

11) Describe how the market segment that a product is targeted at may influence its pricing.

12) Describe the main features of each of the following pricing strategies:
    a) price penetration,
    b) price skimming,
    c) competitive pricing,
    d) cost-plus pricing.

13) What is meant by a company's brand image?

14) Explain how having a strong brand image can benefit a firm.

15) Give one argument for and one argument against choosing to advertise in a magazine rather than in a newspaper.

16) Explain how leaflets and flyers may be used to target a particular market segment.

17) How can firms use sponsorship for promotion?

18) List two sales promotion methods a firm might use to boost sales.

19) Give one advantage and one disadvantage to a firm of using sales promotion.

20) Describe two ways in which social media can be used as a method of promotion.

21) Describe how a company can use someone's internet search history for their advertising.

22) State two factors that will affect the place where a company sells its products.

23) Describe what is meant by an e-tailer.

Methods of Production

Businesses need to work out how to <u>make</u> their products — this is called <u>production</u> or <u>manufacturing</u>. On this page you'll meet <u>job production</u> and <u>flow production</u>, and then <u>batch production</u> is coming up on the next page.

There are Two Ultimate Reasons for Business Operations

1) Business operations generally have one of two <u>main purposes</u>:
   - To <u>produce goods</u>, such as books or cars.
   - To <u>provide services</u>, such as haircuts or eye tests.

2) A business that produces <u>goods</u> has to decide the <u>best way</u> to manufacture its products. There are a number of ways to do this depending on the <u>type</u> of product and the <u>scale</u> of the business operation.

Job Production is Making One Thing at a Time

1) Job production is used when a firm manufactures <u>individual</u>, <u>unique</u> products. Each product has a <u>unique design</u> based upon the <u>customer's specification</u>. Examples include the building of <u>ships</u> and <u>bridges</u>, and handmade crafts such as <u>furniture making</u> and <u>made-to-measure</u> clothes.

2) These products often require highly <u>skilled labour</u> and have a high <u>labour-to-capital ratio</u> (i.e. lots of workers are needed, but relatively little financial investment) — they can be very <u>labour-intensive</u>.

3) As each product is <u>unique</u>, they can take a <u>long time</u> to make. <u>Fewer</u> products are made in a <u>set period of time</u> compared to other production methods, meaning the firm's <u>productivity</u> will be <u>low</u>.

4) The business will generally have <u>high costs</u>, as they'll need <u>skilled workers</u> to produce the goods, who will have <u>higher wages</u> than unskilled workers. Since each product that's made is <u>unique</u>, the company is less able to take advantage of <u>economies of scale</u> e.g. by buying materials in <u>bulk</u>. So their <u>unit costs</u> will be <u>high</u>.

   See p.41 for more on economies of scale.

5) Higher costs mean that a company will need to give its products <u>higher prices</u> in order to make a <u>profit</u>. However, the products are <u>unique</u> and usually <u>high quality</u>, so customers may still buy the products even if the company sets its prices <u>very high</u>, which can lead to <u>higher profits</u> for a firm.

Flow Production is Making Lots of Things Continuously

1) This is the <u>opposite</u> of job production. All products are <u>identical</u> and the aim is to produce as <u>many as possible</u> along an <u>assembly line</u>, and make <u>productivity</u> as high as possible. To be efficient, production has to be <u>continuous</u> with no stoppages — many flow production factories operate 24 hours a day with workers rotating in <u>shifts</u>.

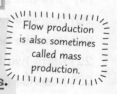

Flow production is also sometimes called mass production.

2) The aim is to gain from <u>economies of scale</u> and so have low <u>average unit costs</u> to allow <u>competitive</u> prices. Modern flow production techniques use <u>robots</u>, not people, to do most of the work. Where workers do have jobs along the assembly line they are <u>simpler tasks</u> than in job production. Flow production is highly <u>capital-intensive</u> (it needs a lot of money — to buy machinery, for example) and may also require a lot of <u>space</u> for product <u>storage</u>.

Shouldn't have had that last cup of tea.

3) It is used for <u>mass-market</u> products. Most modern consumer goods are produced this way — <u>chocolate bars</u>, <u>mobile phones</u>, <u>televisions</u>... etc.

PRACTICE QUESTION

Job production — it'd solve the unemployment crisis...

Q1 Which Stitch is a firm that makes costumes. For a recent play, Which Stitch were asked to make costumes for the five main characters. The theatre company told the design team how they wanted each costume to look and each item was made to their unique requirements. The remaining cast's costumes were bought from a wholesaler (a firm that sells costumes in bulk at low cost).
   a) What method of production does Which Stitch use?
   b) Suggest two reasons why the theatre company didn't use Which Stitch for all of its costumes.

More on Methods of Production

Technology can affect the productivity of a business. I should know — my productivity hasn't been the same since I downloaded Angry Birds™ last month... I have already reached level 306, though...

Batch Production is a Mixture of Job and Flow Production

1) In batch production, firms use flow production techniques to make a batch of one thing then stop, reorganise, and make a batch of something else.

2) It is suited to products that are identical to each other, but which are only produced in limited quantities — or for a limited amount of time. For example, furniture (where producers make a limited number of many different designs).

3) Batch production is faster than job production, since each product in a batch is identical. So firms that use batch production have higher productivity than firms using job production.

4) The company can also buy materials in larger quantities than job production, so can take advantage of economies of scale. This means unit costs are lower than job production, so prices can be lower and therefore more competitive.

5) However, time is needed to change between batches, so productivity is lower than for flow production.

6) Batch production is also more expensive than flow production because, for example, different machinery and tools might be needed to make different products. This means prices might not be as competitive as products made using flow production.

Technology can Affect Production

1) Advances in technology have created new ways to produce goods. For example, robots are now often used instead of human staff for tasks such as assembling products or packing products into boxes. It's usually cheaper and faster for robots to do these jobs instead of humans.

2) Technology can also be used to help design products. For example, computers can be made to design products digitally, and this information can then be fed straight into the production machine. For example, 3D printing can be used to print a prototype (a test model) of a product from a digital file. This is faster and cheaper than traditional methods of making prototypes, making the design process more efficient.

3) There are advantages and disadvantages to using technology:

Advantages

- Technology can carry out processes more quickly and accurately than humans. So using technology can increase the productivity of the business and the goods that are produced should be of a more consistent quality.
- Technology means that machines can work 24/7, so production can be completely continuous.
- In the long term, it's cheaper to run machines than to pay humans to do the same thing.

Disadvantages

- Using technology can be very expensive — it can cost a lot to buy and install new machines and they may need regular maintenance and updates. Staff will also need to be trained to use the technology, which can be expensive and time-consuming.
- Some technologies might replace manual work, so staff might be worried they'll lose their jobs. This could demotivate them, causing their productivity to go down.
- Machines are often only suited to one task, which can make them inflexible. This makes it difficult if the business wants to change its production method (or the product it's making).

Schools (sort of) use batch production — take a look at your batch-mates...

Batch production is what your friendly neighbourhood bakery will do. Think about it... they'll make the dough for one type of bread, bake lots of loaves, and then move on to the next thing. Like iced buns... Mmmm... iced buns...

Managing Stock

Managing stock is really important for a business — the more they have the more it costs to store, but if they have too little then they risk running out. So it's a balancing act to get things just right.

Just-in-Time Keeps Stock Levels as Low as Possible

- Just-in-time (JIT) aims to keep stock levels to the bare minimum — preferably zero.
- Ideally, all raw materials come in one door, are made into products and go straight out another door — all 'just in time' for delivery to customers.
- Computer systems are usually used to calculate stock levels and automatically order more when more supplies are needed.
- The main benefit of JIT is that it reduces the cost of having to keep stock (you need less warehouse space, fewer warehouse workers, and so on).
- It also means stock is less likely to go out of date as it shouldn't be stored for very long.
- JIT helps cash flow, as there won't be much delay between buying supplies and selling the product.
- The main problem is that it requires a lot of coordination between the firm and its suppliers. The firm needs to take lots of frequent deliveries of stock — if any of these deliveries don't arrive on time or there are mistakes with the order, the firm could run out of stock.
- A JIT method also means that firms buy small quantities of stock at a time, rather than buying in bulk. This means they lose out on economies of scale (see page 41).

STORES
Operating on Just-in-Time

We're out of stock again. Good work.

Bar Gate Stock Graphs Show a Company when to Order Materials

1) Some businesses use a production and distribution system where they make sure they have buffer stocks (extra stocks) of items at every stage of the process — from raw materials to finished products — just in case there is a supply shortage or customer demand increases unexpectedly.

2) The main problem is that firms can be left with big stockpiles of items, which can be costly to store.

3) One method to keep control of stock is to use bar gate stock graphs.

4) These graphs monitor how much stock the business has, and show when a business should order more stock so that by the time the new stock has arrived, the business hasn't needed to use its buffer. They also show the maximum amount of stock a business can hold, so that it doesn't order too much.

- Chairs That Rock make wooden furniture. They always need to have nails in stock.
- When stocks of nails fall to 800, they reorder more.
- The hope is that by the time the new stock arrives the stock level won't have fallen below 250 nails. 250 nails is the minimum level of nails the firm always wants to keep — it is their buffer stock level.
- You can use the bar gate stock graph to identify when an order of new nails arrived — it's where the graph is vertical.
- The height of the vertical line shows how many nails were ordered. E.g. on day 12, stock arrives. The stock level rose from 350 nails to 1150 nails. So it ordered 1150 − 350 = 800 nails.
- The amount of time it takes stock to be delivered is the difference between the time where stock is at the reorder level and the time when stock arrives. Here, the first time stock hit the reorder level was on day 6. The stock arrived on day 12, so the delivery time was 12 − 6 = 6 days.

BUSINESS EXAMPLE

Graph — y-axis: Number of nails (1250, 800, 250, 0); x-axis: Time (days) (0, 20, 40). Labels: Maximum level, Reorder level, Minimum level, Reorder here.

'Just-in-time' is not the best approach when it comes to revision...

Most businesses will use computer systems to monitor stock and order more when levels are low — so the right stock should turn up by magic when it's needed. This makes stock control much easier — especially in large firms.

Theme 2: Topic 2.3 — Making Operational Decisions

Working With Suppliers

As you're about to see, getting a firm to run like clockwork isn't just about what goes on inside the firm...

Procurement *and* Logistics *are Really Important* in a Business

1) Procurement means finding and buying things that a firm needs from suppliers outside of the firm. E.g. for a clothes manufacturer, procurement would involve finding and buying the material it needs.

2) Logistics means getting goods or services from one part of the supply chain to another. E.g. a clothes manufacturer would need to have the material it needs transported to its factory.

3) Having effective procurement and logistics systems in place improves the efficiency of a business — the business will have the supplies it needs at the right time. This means, for example, there will be no breaks in production because materials aren't available, or that materials don't have to be wasted because they didn't arrive at the right time or weren't really needed.

4) Effective procurement and logistics can reduce the overall costs of a business. If a business gets its supplies at the best price and it doesn't waste money by being inefficient it will have lower overall costs. This will reduce the unit cost — the amount it costs to make each item. So the firm can make more profit on each item or pass the savings on to the consumer by reducing prices.

5) Well-managed procurement and logistics helps to ensure a firm's products are high-quality, a reasonable price and delivered on time. This improves both customer satisfaction and the firm's reputation.

Companies Need to *Choose* Their Suppliers *Carefully*

One role of procurement is to choose a supplier and build a relationship with them. To choose a supplier, the company should consider the following things:

Quality

- The quality of supplies needs to be consistent.
- Customers can be very selective about quality — the internet means it's easy for them to shop elsewhere if they're not happy with the quality of a product.
- Customers will associate poor quality with the business they buy from, not their suppliers.

Trust

- If a supplier lets a firm down, that firm may not be able to supply its own customers.
- So firms need suppliers they can trust.
- Suppliers need to deliver high-quality products on time, or give plenty of warning if they can't.

Availability

- If a supplier is often out of stock of items, it could affect the firm's production process.
- So they need to make sure their supplier can provide stock in sufficient quantities.

Delivery

- Firms need to consider how much it will cost to get supplies delivered, and how quickly they want supplies to arrive.
- Delivery from a supplier that's near the firm is likely to be cheaper and faster than from a supplier that's further away.
- Delivery should also be reliable — if a supplier doesn't deliver stock on time or it gets damaged along the way, the business's production could be disrupted.

Price (the total cost of getting the product)

- Firms have to decide how much they want to pay for supplies and whether cost is their top priority.
- If they want to cut down the time it takes to serve customers, suppliers that offer faster delivery may rate higher than those that compete on price alone.
- Also, cheaper suppliers will often supply lower quality products. The firm needs to balance reduced costs with the quality of the product or service it wants to provide.

Chinese, Indian, kebab shop — I love choosing my supplier...

If a supplier is late or supplies shoddy goods then it can have serious knock-on effects on the business.

Quality

Even the most productive business in the world won't get far if its products aren't up to scratch.

Customers Expect Quality from All Parts of a Business

1) Products should be good quality, of course. The quality can depend on different factors such as the materials the product is made from and the production method used to assemble the product. At the very least, customers expect products to work properly, and not fall apart straight away.

2) For businesses that provide a service, the service needs to be good quality. For example, a bus company needs to make sure its buses are clean, well-maintained and arrive when they're supposed to.

3) Monitoring quality helps a firm to control its costs. By making sure products are high quality, the firm should waste less from making products that it can't sell and compensating customers who return poor quality items. It should also reduce the cost of customer service, as there should be fewer complaints.

4) If a firm is known for producing good quality items it will improve the firm's brand image. This may give the firm a competitive advantage as customers will be more likely to choose them over competitors. This means the firm may be able to charge more for its items and so could make more profit.

5) Firms need to have good systems in place to make sure their products are high quality — quality control and quality assurance are two systems they can use...

Quality Control Involves Checking For Faults

1) Checking products as they're being made helps to find faults before a product reaches the customer. Products are usually checked by trained quality inspectors at three different stages:

> Check raw materials from suppliers. ⟶ Take random samples to check quality of work in progress. ⟶ Take random samples of finished products and remove items if they're not the right quality.

2) Defects may be spotted before they have finished making the product, reducing waste.

3) The process can be expensive for a firm (sometimes whole batches might need to be scrapped). But the cost would be greater if dissatisfied customers returned products or stopped buying them.

4) Quality control can also be carried out for businesses that provide services, even though there isn't a physical product to check. For example, many shops will employ 'secret shoppers' who visit the stores pretending to be customers, and check that the staff are providing the right quality of service. Staff in stores which have poor quality can then have training to improve their service.

Quality Assurance is about Making Sure Things Don't Go Wrong

1) Quality assurance means checking that quality is being maintained throughout each process involved in making the product. It aims to stop errors from being made in the first place, rather than needing to get rid of faulty goods once they've been made.

2) For example, at each stage of a production line employees should check that the work they pass on to the next stage is good quality.

3) A firm can have its quality assessed by an external body. It may be awarded a rating or certificate that it can display to assure customers that the business provides high quality products.

> **BUSINESS EXAMPLE**
>
> 1) VisitEngland is a company that recommends holiday ideas in the UK.
> 2) Among other things, VisitEngland assess visitor attractions and awards them a star rating based on the quality of the whole experience — from promotional material to the visit itself.
> 3) The attraction can use its VisitEngland star rating to attract customers, e.g. by displaying it on its website, leaflets, etc. This encourages the attraction to have high quality in all parts of the firm.

Quality — my parents had that sussed when they created me...

Q1 Partee Maxx is a business that organises events.
Explain why having a quality control system may give them a competitive advantage.

Theme 2: Topic 2.3 — Making Operational Decisions

The Sales Process

At the end of the day, almost every business out there needs to sell a product, so knowing how to sell products is kind of important. So important in fact that there's two lovely pages all about sales coming up...

Customers Want Good Service Throughout the Sales Process

A sales process might involve these steps:

- Finding potential new customers — e.g. a company selling jet skis could have a stand at a boat show. They could ask people to leave contact details if they'd be interested in knowing more about jet skis.
- Approaching potential customers — e.g. calling people who left their contact details at the boat show and inviting them into the showroom.
- Assessing the customer's needs — e.g. finding out what sort of jet ski the person might want.
- Presenting — e.g. showing a customer a suitable jet ski in the showroom, telling them all about it and persuading them to buy one.
- Closing — e.g. getting the customer to formally agree to buying a jet ski (i.e. hand over their cash).
- Follow-up — e.g. calling the customer after the sale to check they are happy with their new jet ski.

Firms should provide great customer service throughout the sales process. Ways of doing this include:

1) Having Excellent Product Knowledge

1) Anyone in a firm involved in the sales process should know the firm's products inside out.
2) This is important for several reasons. For example:

   - Any questions customers have can be answered quickly and accurately.
   - Staff can make sure the customer is getting the product most suited to their needs, and may be able to sell them additional products to go with their initial purchase.
   - The customer feels more confident buying from the firm — if staff seem like they don't really know what they're talking about, the customer may be wary about buying from them.

2) Engaging Well with the Customer

1) Firms should ensure that any experience customers have with them is as positive as possible.
2) This involves staff being polite and friendly with customers and making them feel important and valued. Customers shouldn't feel like they're being pushed into making a purchase, nor should they feel like sales staff aren't listening to what they want in a product.
3) Firms often think of extra ways to make the experience for the customer more positive, such as offering free refreshments or next-day delivery.

You'll never find a better sail than this, Capt'n

3) Having Quick and Efficient Service

1) The sales process should be quick and easy for a customer.
2) For example, the company should quickly answer any questions the customer has.
3) The sales process should also be efficient — this can be achieved by cutting down the number of steps it takes for a customer to get in touch with a company or to buy a product.
4) For example, sales people might be given authority to offer discounts to customers without needing to approve them with a manager first (which would take time).

She sells sea shells at the sea shore...

...and with her excellent product knowledge, the sea shells that she sells are sea shells, I'm sure.

More on The Sales Process

The sales process isn't as easy as 1, 2, 3... Oh no. Coming up are even more things a company should think about doing to make their customers happy and why happy customers are so important.

4) Offering Post-Sales Service

Providing good customer service doesn't end when the sale is complete.
The firm needs to be available for their customers afterwards as well.

- The firm may offer user training — teaching the customer how to use the product they've bought.
- Some businesses have a specific after-sales helpline — customers can contact this to help resolve any issues they have with the product, e.g. if it's not working as they expected.
- Some products, like cars and boilers, might need to be serviced throughout their lifespan — firms can often do this for their customers.

5) Responding to Customer Feedback

1) Customers might give feedback to a business if they've had a particularly good or bad experience. This could be private feedback, e.g. an e-mail, or public feedback, such as an online review. The business may even ask the customer for feedback about their experience, e.g. to ask why the customer didn't buy from the business, or to ask how their experience could have been improved.

2) To make a customer feel their views are valued, companies should reply to the feedback. Their responses should be polite — even if the company disagrees with what the customer has said. They should also respond specifically to the comments, rather than giving a generic response. They might even offer a gift in thanks for the feedback, such as a discount on their next purchase.

3) This is particularly important for public feedback, as other potential customers might be influenced by how a business responds.

4) The business can use customer feedback to make changes to the business in order to improve the sales process for future customers.

Providing Good Customer Service is Really Important

Benefits of Good Customer Service

1) Good customer service leads to high levels of customer satisfaction.
2) Satisfied customers are more likely to remain loyal to the company and make repeat purchases from them in the future.
3) Customers may be persuaded to spend more with a company that provides them with good customer service.

Dangers of Poor Customer Service

1) If a company provides poor customer service they're likely to have dissatisfied customers.
2) People like to tell others about poor customer service they have received. The business ends up with a poor brand image so customers will be less loyal, and may buy from other companies. This leads to a lower market share and lower sales.

Good customer service costs money — e.g. the wages of extra staff, and costs of providing after-sales care. But customer service is crucial — most firms recognise that the benefits of customer service outweigh the costs, and ultimately increase profitability.

Not all customers need a good service — some just need a lie down...

Providing good customer service is really important. For example, a coffee shop might serve the best cup of coffee in the whole world, but if the staff all laugh at your hair and won't give you a clean spoon, you might not go back.

Business Calculations

Businesses have to keep a keen eye on their finances. They can find out how <u>risky</u> an <u>investment</u> is likely to be working out the <u>ARR</u>. They can find <u>how much</u> the business is <u>making</u> by working out its <u>gross</u> or <u>net profit</u>.

You Can Find the *Average Rate of Return* on an *Investment*

1) The <u>return</u> on an investment is how much a business <u>makes</u> or <u>loses</u> as a <u>proportion</u> of the <u>original investment</u> that it puts in.

2) You need to be able to work out the <u>average rate of return</u> (<u>ARR</u>).

3) The average rate of return is a calculation of the <u>average return</u> on an investment each year over its <u>lifespan</u>.

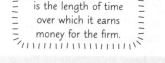
An investment's lifespan is the length of time over which it earns money for the firm.

4) To calculate it you first have to work out the <u>average annual profit</u> — you can do that using this formula:

$$\text{average annual profit} = \frac{\text{total profit}}{\text{number of years}}$$

$$\text{ARR (\%)} = \frac{\text{average annual profit}}{\text{cost of investment}} \times 100$$

5) Then you can put your value for average annual profit into this formula, to find the <u>ARR</u>.

6) Just to be nice, here's a worked example of how to find the ARR:

> **BUSINESS EXAMPLE**
>
> The table below shows the <u>investment</u> that a business made in a project that lasted 5 years. It also shows the <u>profit</u> the business made <u>each year</u> as a result of the investment. Calculate the <u>average rate of return</u> (<u>ARR</u>) for the investment.
>
> | Investment | Yr 1 | Yr 2 | Profit Yr 3 | Yr 4 | Yr 5 |
> |---|---|---|---|---|---|
> | (£10m) | £4m | £5m | £6m | £7m | £5m |
>
> 1) First calculate the <u>total profit</u> of the project — this is the sum of the profit made by the project each year minus the cost of the <u>initial investment</u>: $4 + 5 + 6 + 7 + 5 - 10 = \underline{£17m}$
>
> 2) Then divide the total profit of the project by its lifespan in years to find the <u>average annual profit</u>: $17m \div 5 = \underline{£3.4m}$
>
> 3) Next, you use the <u>formula</u> above to find the <u>ARR</u>: $\quad \text{ARR (\%)} = \frac{\text{average annual profit}}{\text{cost of investment}} \times 100 = \frac{3.4}{10} \times 100 = 34\%$

7) The <u>bigger</u> the ARR for an investment, the <u>more successful</u> the investment for the business. But a good ARR will depend on the <u>firm</u> involved, as well as the <u>amount</u> of money invested — an ARR of <u>6%</u> would be a significant return for a £1m investment, but probably not for a £100 one.

You Need to be Able to Calculate *Gross Profit* and *Net Profit*

1) A business can calculate its <u>net profit</u> and <u>gross profit</u> from its financial data.

2) <u>Gross profit</u> is the profit a firm makes after the cost of <u>making products</u> (the <u>cost of sales</u>) is taken into account. <u>Net profit</u> is the profit a firm makes when <u>all expenses</u> (that includes the <u>operating expenses</u>, e.g. salaries and rent, the <u>interest paid</u> on loans <u>and</u> the <u>cost of sales</u>) are taken into account.

3) Before calculating any kind of profit, it's important to know what the <u>revenue</u> (see p.13) is. This is the total amount of money earned by the business through <u>sales of products</u> in the given time period — you can <u>calculate</u> it using the following equation: $\quad \text{revenue} = \text{sales price} \times \text{quantity sold}$

This can also be called the <u>sales volume</u>.

4) To calculate the <u>gross profit</u>, take away the <u>cost of sales</u> from the <u>revenue</u>: $\quad \text{gross profit} = \text{revenue} - \text{cost of sales}$

5) To calculate the <u>net profit</u>, you can use the following formula: $\quad \text{net profit} = \text{gross profit} - (\text{operating expenses} + \text{interest})$

The total profit calculated for the business example above is really the net profit for the business.

PRACTICE QUESTION

My average rate of return to the fridge is about 20 minutes...

Q1 Calculate the average rate of return for a project in which a company invests £14m and earns back a total of £26m over three years.

More on Business Calculations

You covered a little bit on <u>gross</u> and <u>net profit</u> on the previous page. Now, just to throw some more numbers at you, here's a page on <u>profitability ratios</u>. These show what happens to <u>each pound</u> spent by a customer.

Gross Profit Margin *Ignores Indirect Costs*

Gross profit margin is the <u>fraction</u> of every pound spent by customers that doesn't go directly towards making a product:

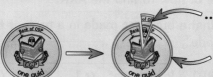

> Gross profit margin = gross profit ÷ sales (revenue) × 100

Here's how to <u>calculate</u> the gross profit margin using this equation:

1) Yummo Chocolates makes and sells chocolates. In 2019, its gross profit was <u>£167 000</u> and its revenue was <u>£180 000</u>.

2) This means the <u>gross profit margin</u> was:

3) Or, if you prefer, you can think of it like this...

> 167 000 ÷ 180 000 = 0.92777...
> 0.92777... × 100 = <u>92.78%</u> (2 d.p.)

For every £1 spent by <u>customers</u>...

...<u>7.22p</u> was used to <u>make</u> the product...

...leaving <u>92.78p</u> — but this still has to pay for <u>expenses</u> like salaries, interest, and so on.

BUSINESS EXAMPLE

What counts as a <u>good</u> gross profit margin depends on the <u>type of business</u>, but the <u>higher</u> the percentage the better. The margin can be <u>improved</u> by <u>increasing prices</u> or reducing the <u>direct cost</u> of sales. Some businesses (e.g. a supermarket chain) can have a <u>low</u> gross profit margin because they sell in <u>high volumes</u> and they need to keep their prices <u>competitive</u> to survive.

Net Profit Margin *Takes All Costs into Account*

<u>Net profit margin</u> is the fraction of every pound spent by customers that the company gets to <u>keep</u> (after all its costs have been paid):

> Net profit margin = net profit ÷ sales (revenue) × 100

1) In 2019, Yummo Chocolates had operating expenses of <u>£147 000</u> and the interest it paid on loans totalled <u>£2000</u>. Its gross profit was <u>£167 000</u>, which meant that it had a net profit of <u>£18 000</u> (£167 000 − £147 000 − £2000).

2) The revenue in 2019 was £180 000, so the <u>net profit margin</u> was:

> 18 000 ÷ 180 000 = 0.1
> 0.1 × 100 = <u>10%</u>

BUSINESS EXAMPLE

For every £1 spent by <u>customers</u>...

...the company gets <u>10p</u> as <u>net profit</u>.

1.11p (= 2000 ÷ 180 000) paid off interest

7.22p was spent making the product (see above)

81.67p (= 147 000 ÷ 180 000) paid off other expenses (e.g. salaries)

Just like for gross profit margins, what counts as a <u>good</u> net profit margin depends on the <u>business</u>, but the <u>higher</u> it is, the <u>better</u>. Net profit margin is often <u>larger</u> for <u>new companies</u> which are still small and don't have many <u>indirect costs</u>. As businesses <u>grow</u>, these costs <u>go up</u> and net profit margin <u>decreases</u>.

PRACTICE QUESTION

Gross profit — it's a disgusting amount of money...

Q1 A business makes £200 000 in revenue in one year. Its cost of sales for the year is £40 000. Calculate the business's gross profit margin. (Hint: the formula for gross profit is on the previous page.)

Business Data and Performance

Businesses collect a lot of information as they go along, about their own and their competitors' finances, their customers and the market in general. It's not just for fun though, all that information comes in handy...

Data Can Help a Business to Make Decisions

1) Businesses have to keep track of how well they are doing. They also need to be able to predict the effect of making certain decisions. Different types of data can help inform a business on the impact of a decision, and so help to support or justify it, or prevent the business from making a mistake.

2) The following types of data may be used by businesses when making decisions:

- Financial data — e.g. cash flow forecasts (p.16-17) can show whether or not a business decision (e.g. investing cash in new equipment) would lead to cash flow problems. Calculations of profit and loss (p.13) and profitability ratios (see previous page) can help a business to see if it should reduce costs or try to increase revenue. And predicting the average rate of return (p.65) of an investment can help a business to determine if an investment would be worthwhile.

- Marketing data — both primary and secondary market research data (p.6) can give an indication of how customer preferences are changing over time. So a business can use this data to see if a business decision is likely to lead to increased sales.

- Market data — e.g. knowing the market share of different businesses, the costs of supplies and prices of competitor products may help a business to see if it should, e.g. lower its prices, or reduce the cost of its supplies.

There are Some Limitations to Financial Data

1) As you saw above, there are lots of different types of financial data that can be used to understand how well a business is performing, and make decisions about the running of the business.

2) In order to use some types of financial data, it's important that there is another source of appropriate data to allow a comparison. For example, a firm could compare how their financial data has changed over time, or they could compare it against a competitor who produces similar products.

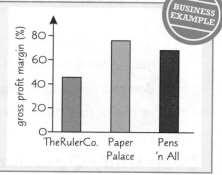

BUSINESS EXAMPLE

1) TheRulerCo. is a company that makes and sells stationery.

2) It uses the bar chart on the right to compare its financial performance with two of its competitors.

3) The bar chart shows that TheRulerCo. has a lower gross profit margin than two of its competitors. So either its cost of sales is higher, or it is charging relatively less for its products.

4) This will mean that TheRulerCo. will be able to make decisions about certain parts of the business, e.g. reducing the cost of raw materials, to help improve its profit margins.

3) However, using financial data to understand business performance isn't perfect. In some cases it may not be possible to directly compare two different sources of data. For example, one firm in the comparison may be much larger or operate in a different country.

4) Even if the same firm's financial performance for different years is compared, it can still be hard to tell exactly what may have caused any changes. That's because there are often lots of different variables which may affect a company's financial performance — such as how well the economy is doing.

5) Another limitation to using financial data to assess business performance is that it only includes quantitative data and not qualitative data (see p.7). Qualitative data can include things like customers' opinions, which can be useful for determining what changes a business should make.

Business performance — it ain't no song and dance...

Using financial data isn't foolproof as you can see, but without it businesses wouldn't be able to get much of an idea of their performance. Businesses can use their financial data alongside other forms of data such as market research, to get a more well-rounded idea of how their business is performing compared to their competitors.

Case Study — Topics 2.3 & 2.4

Businesses have to work really hard to make sure the company runs smoothly — and all while trying to make a profit. See if you can apply what you've learnt in Topics 2.3 and 2.4 to a real business example.

Business Report: Making Operational and Financial Decisions

Marks and Spencer plc

Marks and Spencer plc is a large, British retailer with around 900 stores in the UK and over 400 stores overseas, including in other parts of Europe and in Asia. It is well-known for providing customers with high quality goods. In the year ending April 2015, Marks and Spencer had UK sales of £9222.1 m and a gross profit in the UK of £3817.4 m.

Marks and Spencer works closely with the factories that supply it with products. Each factory must meet minimum standards set by Marks and Spencer, otherwise they risk having their orders cancelled and no longer being used as a supplier. For example, one of the minimum standards is that each batch of products made in a factory must have a batch card. This card should detail all the processes that the product has been through in the factory, whether the product was received in good condition at each stage, and whether each process was completed satisfactory. It also includes the name of the worker that was in charge of each process.

Marks and Spencer encourages the factories that supply its products to use a 'just-in-time' method of stock control. One way they get factories to see how well they're doing at this is by asking them to monitor the length of time between raw materials arriving at the factory and the finished products that use these materials being sent out.

Case Study Questions

Think about all the different things you've learnt in the previous two topics to answer the following questions.

1) Explain how Marks and Spencer's use of suppliers may affect its competitiveness.
2) Calculate Marks and Spencer's UK gross profit margin in the year ending April 2015. Give your answer to one decimal place.
3) Explain how the use of batch cards is an example of quality assurance.
4) Explain why batch production would be a suitable method for a factory that makes clothes for Marks and Spencer.
5) Analyse the impact of encouraging the use of just-in-time stock control on Marks and Spencer's gross profit margin.

On your Marks (and Spencer's)...

... get learning. Getting a business to run smoothly isn't just about getting things working well on the inside of the business. There are also external things to think about, such as choosing just the right supplier.

Revision Summary — Topics 2.3 & 2.4

Now for a bumper edition of revision summary questions. Cast your mind back to Topic 2.3 for the first lot (if those pesky calculations haven't yet clogged your brain cells) then go on to the juicy questions for Topic 2.4.

1) a) What is meant by 'job production'?
   b) Give an example of a product made by job production.
2) a) What is meant by 'flow production'?
   b) Give an example of a product made by flow production.
3) Give one advantage of flow production over job production.
4) What is meant by 'batch production'?
5) Explain one way using technology in the production process can improve productivity.
6) What is meant by a just-in-time (JIT) method of stock control?
7) Give one advantage of using a JIT method of stock control.
8) Explain how a business can use a bar gate stock graph to manage its supplies.
9) What does procurement mean?
10) What does logistics mean?
11) Give three important factors that a business should consider when choosing a supplier.
12) Explain two reasons why it's good for a business to ensure customers get products that are good quality.
13) Describe the difference between quality control and quality assurance.
14) Explain one reason why having good product knowledge allows sales staff to provide good customer service.
15) Give one way in which sales staff could make sure they engage positively with their customers.
16) Give one example of a post-sales service that a business might offer their customers.
17) Explain why a business should always respond to customer feedback.
18) Explain why providing good customer service is important for customer loyalty.
19) Explain how poor customer service could lead to a big fall in a firm's revenue.
20) Write the equation for finding the average rate of return for an investment.
21) Describe the difference between gross profit and net profit.
22) a) What does the net profit margin represent?
    b) How is the net profit margin calculated?
23) Give three different types of financial data that a business might use to inform business decisions.
24) Explain how market research data might be used to support a business decision.
25) Give two types of market data which may be used by a business to inform a business decision.
26) Explain why it may sometimes be difficult to directly compare financial data from different companies.

Internal Organisational Structures

There could be thousands of employees inside a business — like little minions running around, doing someone's bidding... The internal organisational structure is how all of these people are organised inside the business.

Organisational Structures Organise People

1) It's important that a firm has a clear internal organisational structure. This makes it easy for everybody in the business to know who is responsible for what, and helps the company to make sure that it has people in every job role to deal with each of its activities.

The number of people on each layer generally increases as you go down the organisational structure.

2) Most firms have layers in their organisational structure.

3) There are four basic roles of staff, with different responsibilities, that make up the layers:

- DIRECTORS are responsible for the business's strategy (its overall direction). The directors decide on strategy and targets at regular board meetings.
- SENIOR MANAGERS organise the carrying out of the directors' strategy. A large firm may have middle and junior managers ranked below the senior managers.
- SUPERVISORS or TEAM LEADERS are ranked below managers. They usually look after specific projects or small teams of operational or support staff.
- OPERATIONAL and SUPPORT STAFF are workers who aren't responsible for other staff. They're often given specific tasks to perform by managers, supervisors or team leaders.

4) The directors are on the top layer of an organisational structure, and operational and support staff are on the lowest layer.

5) The chain connecting directors to operational and support staff is called the chain of command.

6) At each level, a certain amount of responsibility is delegated (passed on) to people in the level below.

7) The span of control is the number of workers who report to one manager.

An Organisational Structure can be *Hierarchical* or *Flat*

1) A hierarchical organisational structure has more layers than a flat organisational structure. In a flat structure there are very few (if any) layers between directors and operational and support staff.

2) Whether a firm's structure is hierarchical or flat will affect communication and management in the firm:

There's more about communication within a firm on p.72.

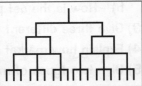

Hierarchical Structures

- There is a long chain of command with more layers of management.
- This can make communication between the top and bottom of the structure difficult and slow because more people need to pass on the message.
- Each manager only has a narrow span of control. This can make a firm more effective as managers can monitor the employees they are responsible for more closely.

Flat Structures

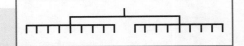

- There is a short chain of command. This means that messages can be passed on quickly.
- However, each manager also has a wide span of control. This means that each manager has to manage a lot of employees at once — it can be difficult to manage a lot of employees effectively.

Sofa in front of the TV — that's my internal organisation sorted...

PRACTICE QUESTION

Q1 KS Dentistry Ltd.'s flat organisational structure has become a hierarchical structure. Explain one disadvantage to KS Dentistry Ltd. of having a hierarchical structure rather than a flat structure.

More On Internal Organisational Structures

Firms need to decide how much power to give to people at each layer of their organisational structures.

Organisations can be *Centralised* or *Decentralised*

How much power and authority is delegated at each layer in an organisational structure
will depend on whether the bosses want a centralised or decentralised structure.

Centralised Organisations

1) All major decisions are made by one person or a few senior managers at the top of the structure.

2) Advantages are that these senior managers tend to have plenty of experience, and can get an overview of the whole business. Policies will be uniform throughout the business.

3) On the downside, if all decisions need to be made by one or two people, it can slow down decision-making and communication of decisions can take a long time to filter through to employees. This means that the organisation reacts slowly to change.

4) Senior managers at the top of the organisational structure can become very powerful. But depending too heavily on a few people at the top can cause problems if those people lack specialist knowledge or if they 'lose their touch' and start making poor decisions.

Decentralised Organisations

1) The authority to make most decisions is shared out — for example, power might be delegated to regional managers or to more junior employees in individual branches of a business.

2) Advantages are that employees can use expert knowledge of their sector to make decisions. They don't always need to communicate these decisions with managers above them for approval, so changes can be made more quickly. This is really important in competitive environments, where a firm needs to respond to changes or opportunities in the market more quickly than its competitors.

3) Another advantage is that senior managers at the top of the organisational structure are not responsible for making as many decisions. This means there's less need for a central office where decisions are made (a headquarters), which can decrease a firm's fixed costs (see p.13).

4) The disadvantages are that inconsistencies may develop between departments or regions. Also, the decision-makers might not be able to see the overall needs of the business.

BUSINESS EXAMPLE

1) Supermarket chains (e.g. Tesco, Asda) have a decentralised structure.

2) Big decisions on things such as branding and marketing campaigns are made by directors at the top of the organisational structure.

3) But each store usually has its own manager who makes important decisions about the running of their store, e.g. decisions about recruiting and training staff, and controlling stock levels.

Businesses Need to Choose the *Most Appropriate* Structure

1) The type of organisational structure a business has depends on many things, e.g. the business's size.

2) A small business is likely to have a flat structure — it's often just run by the owner without the need for any additional managers.

3) As the business grows and employs more staff, managers might be needed to help organise and control things, so the organisational structure becomes hierarchical.

4) The bigger the business, the greater the number of managers needed (and the greater the costs). A big business might be easier to operate if it splits into different parts (e.g. different regions).

5) Businesses often start with a centralised structure, but decentralise as they get too big to make all the decisions at the top or if it's better for different areas of the business to be managed separately.

Decentralisation — popular in the doughnut industry...

Make sure you understand why some firms prefer to have a centralised structure, while others choose to decentralise.

Communication

Communication is <u>very important</u> in business — it involves more than just having a natter at the water cooler.

Firms Have to Overcome *Barriers* to Communicate Effectively

1) <u>Effective communication</u> in a business is <u>really important</u> — it means that <u>different areas</u> of the business <u>work well</u> together, and that <u>everyone</u> in the business knows <u>what</u> they should be doing and <u>why</u>. It can <u>improve staff motivation</u> as staff will know <u>what's going on</u> in the firm and are likely to feel more <u>confident</u> that they're <u>doing their job properly</u>.

The report will be done by Monday.

2) In order to communicate effectively, <u>messages</u> need to <u>reach</u> the people that need to <u>receive</u> them without unnecessary <u>delay</u> and without being <u>misinterpreted</u>.

3) Firms need to overcome <u>barriers to communication</u> in order to communicate effectively. These include:

She bought a gun on Sunday??

- <u>Noise</u> — it's difficult to hold a conversation in a <u>noisy environment</u>, such as a busy factory.
- <u>Personalities</u> — some employees may feel <u>uncomfortable</u> communicating with other people in the firm because, e.g. they <u>don't get on</u> personally or feel they are <u>unapproachable</u>.
- <u>Distance</u> — many businesses operate across <u>different sites</u>, sometimes <u>many miles</u> apart, so it can be difficult to speak to people <u>face-to-face</u>.
- <u>Jargon</u> — <u>technical language</u> used in <u>one department</u> may not be <u>understood</u> by people in <u>other</u> departments.

Face-to-face is one of the most effective ways to communicate — body language can help express the message and it's easy to confirm the message has been properly received and understood.

Too Little *or* Too Much Communication Can Cause Problems

Businesses need to get the <u>balance</u> right between having <u>insufficient</u> (not enough) and <u>excessive</u> (too much) communication.

Insufficient Communication

1) <u>Insufficient communication</u> can lead to <u>inefficiency</u>. People may be <u>slow</u> to receive important messages about what they <u>should be doing</u>, meaning <u>time</u> and <u>money</u> is <u>wasted</u> on them doing things <u>incorrectly</u>. It may also mean that information <u>isn't</u> passed on between different <u>departments</u> or <u>teams</u> — this may mean that some tasks end up getting done <u>more than once</u>, or are not done in ways that are <u>best</u> for the business as a whole.

2) Insufficient communication can <u>demotivate</u> staff. They may feel <u>frustrated</u> if a lack of communication is stopping them from doing their <u>job properly</u>. Also, they may not feel <u>valued</u> if they're <u>not told</u> about things that are going on in the firm.

There's more on why it's important to keep staff motivated on page 76.

Excessive Communication

1) <u>Excessive communication</u> can lead to <u>inefficiency</u>. It takes <u>time</u> to <u>pass on</u> and <u>receive</u> messages — if people are frequently involved in communication about things that don't <u>directly affect them</u> it can <u>waste</u> valuable time. People may also start to take <u>less notice</u> of messages, and <u>miss out</u> ones that are important to them.

2) Excessive communication may mean many people are trying to pass on the same message — employees may get <u>conflicting information</u> from different sources and there may be <u>confusion</u> over which information is <u>correct</u>. This can lead to <u>time</u> being <u>wasted</u> while the workers find out the correct information, or <u>mistakes</u> being made while workers follow the <u>wrong</u> information. Both of these things reduce <u>efficiency</u> and <u>productivity</u>, which can reduce <u>output</u>.

3) Staff may feel <u>demotivated</u> by excessive communication — they may feel <u>overwhelmed</u> with all the information they are receiving and <u>annoyed</u> if it's affecting their ability to do their <u>job well</u>.

Thumping people you don't like = bad communication...

Poor communication can lead to inefficient and badly-motivated employees — and that's never gonna end well.

Ways of Working

All employees have a contract of employment — a legal agreement between themselves and their employer. The contract includes details about the way the employee works, e.g. how many hours they are required to do.

Employment Can be Full-Time or Part-Time

1) Working full-time usually means around 35-40 hours a week. Part-time staff work 'less than a full working week' — usually between 10 and 30 hours per week.

2) Some people prefer to have a full-time job, or need to work full-time for financial reasons. Other people work part-time so they can spend more time with family or on other interests.

3) There are pros and cons of both types of employment for businesses. Full-time staff are good if there's enough work for them to do, since they are likely to have only one job and so the business will have more control over the hours they work. But employing staff part-time can make more financial sense if a business is only really busy at certain periods. It also means they can fill in when other staff members are absent (e.g. due to sickness or holidays).

Staff Can Work Flexible Hours

1) Employees that have been with a firm for at least 26 weeks can request to work flexibly — this is when working hours and patterns are adapted to suit the employee. E.g. a full-time employee might be allowed to work their 37 hours over four days, rather than the usual five days. This can be very motivating for staff as it makes it easier to fit other commitments around their working life.

2) Some employees have zero hour contracts — this means that the employer doesn't have to offer them any work at all. Nor does the employee have to accept any work that is offered to them. The contracts are used in businesses where there can be lots of fluctuation in demand, e.g. hotels. They are a cheap form of labour for businesses — they don't waste money paying staff when they're not really needed.

Employees Can be Permanent, Temporary or Freelance

1) A permanent contract of employment has no end date. The person stays at the firm unless: (i) they choose to leave,   (ii) they're dismissed for misconduct,   (iii) their job is made redundant.

2) A temporary contract is for a fixed period (e.g. six months, one year, or whatever). At the end of the period, the contract can be renewed, or the person can leave the company.

3) A freelance contract is when a self-employed person is recruited by a company, usually to work on a specific project. Freelancers can usually be hired and dismissed at short notice.

4) Temporary and freelance contracts can make it easier for the firm to employ people with particular skills for a particular period (without the commitment of a permanent contract). This can make it easier to adjust the number of staff according to the needs of the business.

Technology Has Had an Impact on the Ways Employees Work

1) Advances in technology have made processes more efficient — e.g. many repetitive tasks can be done much faster and more accurately by computers than by staff. Working with technology is now a much bigger part of people's jobs, which has changed the way many people work.

2) Technology has made it easier for employees to share information and communicate with each other. E.g. documents can be put onto a firm's intranet so they can be accessed by employees in any location at any time (as long as they have an internet connection), employees can communicate via emails and video calls, and mobile devices allow people to communicate from many different locations.

3) This has impacted on the ways that people work. E.g. it's easier for employees to work remotely (i.e. in locations away from their employers' offices, such as at home or on a beach in the Maldives).

I'm very flexible — one of those zero hour contracts will suit me fine...

There's lots to learn on this page — see if you can write a mini-essay about the different ways of working.

Recruitment

Recruitment is the process of finding that special someone — that is, the best person to do a job. Businesses need to recruit people to increase their size, to gain new people with expertise or to replace staff that have left.

Businesses Need to Be Clear About the Job on Offer

There are several steps involved in recruitment — job analysis, advertisement and selection.

1) Job analysis is where a firm thinks in depth about every little detail of the job in question.

2) The business then advertises the job. This usually includes two documents — a job description and a person specification, which are produced from the job analysis.

- Job description — includes the formal title of the job, the main purpose of the job, the main duties plus any occasional duties. It will also state who the job holder will report to, and whether they will be responsible for any other staff.
- Person specification — lists the qualifications, experience, skills and attitudes needed for the job.

3) Then the business has to go through the candidates that apply and select the best one.

A Firm can Recruit People Internally or Externally

The purpose of a job advert is to get as many suitable people as possible to apply for the job. Firms can use job adverts to recruit internally or externally:

- INTERNAL RECRUITMENT involves recruiting current employees into new roles. The job position is advertised within the company.
- The advantages are that it's much cheaper, the post can be filled more quickly, the candidates will already know a lot about the firm, and bosses may already know the candidate well.
- On the downside, there will be no 'new blood' or new ideas, and the employee's move will leave a vacancy to fill.

- EXTERNAL RECRUITMENT involves recruiting from outside the business. The job can be advertised in lots of places, e.g. the local and national press, job centres, trade journals and employment websites.
- An advantage is that the job advert will be seen by more people, so it's more likely that the firm will find somebody really suited to the job.
- However, advertising externally isn't cheap — only specialist and senior jobs get advertised in the national press because it's very expensive.

The business's needs determine which method of recruitment they use. E.g. internal recruitment may be used for a job which requires an in-depth knowledge of the firm's processes, whereas external recruitment may be used if a lot of new recruits are needed at once or no one in the firm has suitable qualifications.

CVs and Application Forms Help a Firm Select the Best Candidate

Most firms ask candidates to send a written application for a job — these are used to decide who to interview.

1) A curriculum vitae (CV) is a summary of a person's personal details, skills, qualifications and interests. It's written in a standard format to give the firm the basic facts. Almost all firms ask for a CV.

2) Many businesses also ask candidates to fill in an application form. These forms give the firm the information it wants — and nothing else. This means they're much quicker to process and more relevant to the job than open-ended letters written by the candidates.

3) Many companies now like to use online application forms, where applicants fill in their details on the company's website. This allows the company to compare the applications using computer software.

PRACTICE QUESTION

Lonely business WLTM right person for ~~cuddles~~ hard graft...

Q1 A furniture manufacturer is recruiting staff for a new showroom. An advert for the role has been put up on noticeboards around the furniture factory. The advert includes a person specification.
   a) Outline what a person specification is.
   b) Give two advantages of the firm advertising the role internally rather than externally.

Training and Development

Training employees helps them to keep developing their skills, so they can be brilliant at their jobs.

There are Different Types of Training

1) Staff need training when they start working for a company so that they know how to do their job.

2) But even when they've been working for a company for a while, employees still need ongoing training. This could be to retrain them so they learn new processes or how to use new technology, or just to help them develop so that they're doing their job as well as possible.

3) Many firms plan the training they want their employees to have, but in some firms employees are encouraged to self-learn — this is where employees seek out their own training and development. E.g. they might be given access to online videos, apps and courses which teach different skills. They can pick and choose what they want to learn depending on where they want to take their career.

Training can be Informal...

1) Informal training is usually done 'on-the-job' — the employee learns to do their job better by being shown how to do it, and then practising.

2) There is no strict plan to the training and it is usually given by other workers.

3) It's cost-effective for the employer because the employee works and learns at the same time.

4) A problem is that bad working practices may be passed on.

...Or Formal

1) Formal training often involves a set plan with learning objectives and a schedule.

2) The training can involve learning in a firm's training department or away from the workplace, e.g. at a local college.

3) It's more expensive than informal training, but it's often higher quality because it's usually taught by people who are better qualified to train others.

Performance Reviews Help Employees to Develop

Performance reviews can also play a part in employees' training and development — this is when firms set employees targets and then review their performance to make sure they're developing as they should. E.g.:

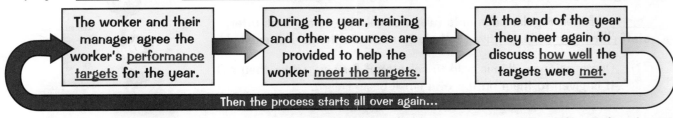

| The worker and their manager agree the worker's performance targets for the year. | During the year, training and other resources are provided to help the worker meet the targets. | At the end of the year they meet again to discuss how well the targets were met. |

Then the process starts all over again...

People who meet or beat their targets may be rewarded with higher pay or a promotion. If a worker doesn't meet their targets, the manager can decide what training or support they might need to help them improve.

Training and Development has Many Benefits

1) Training and development can make staff more productive — it makes staff better at their jobs, which means they may work faster. This could lower the business's unit costs (see next page).

2) Training can help staff stay up to date with changes in the business, such as knowing how to use new technology.

3) Overall, training and development is likely to make staff feel motivated — it shows the firm is interested in how well staff are doing their jobs and are willing to help them improve, and it makes staff feel like they're progressing in the firm. This might increase staff retention — see next page.

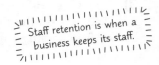
Staff retention is when a business keeps its staff.

'Bruno... Fetch me my slippers!' Sorry, just trying to train my Staffie...

Good training motivates staff, which may make them work harder and be more likely to stay in a firm. Happy days.

Motivation

This page covers some <u>financial methods</u> for <u>motivating</u> staff. Basically, the more <u>money</u> you give people, the more <u>valued</u> they'll feel and the <u>happier</u> they'll be doing their job — who'd've thought...

Motivated Staff are More Productive

1) Motivated staff work harder, which leads to <u>high productivity</u> — workers want the firm to do well and so do their jobs as <u>well</u> as they can to help this happen.

2) Staff who are <u>motivated</u> and <u>happy</u> in their jobs are more likely to <u>stay</u> with the firm. Having a high level of <u>staff retention</u> is good for a firm as it means less <u>time</u> and <u>money</u> is spent having to recruit and train new workers, which <u>reduces</u> the firm's <u>costs</u>.

3) Having highly motivated staff may also <u>attract new employees</u> to the firm. This makes recruiting new staff <u>easier</u> because there are likely to be <u>lots of applicants</u> for vacancies.

> Being more productive means staff can produce goods faster or using fewer resources. This reduces the unit cost of each item produced.

Financial Motivation can be Wages or a Salary

1) Most people get <u>remuneration</u> (payment) for the <u>work</u> they do for an employer (some people might not, e.g. if they're doing <u>voluntary</u> work).

2) Often, the <u>more</u> that a worker is paid, the <u>more motivated</u> they feel to do their job.

3) Workers can be paid with <u>wages</u> or with a <u>salary</u>.

4) <u>Wages</u> are commonly paid <u>weekly or monthly</u> — usually to <u>manual</u> workers. The <u>amount paid</u> is based on the <u>amount of work</u> that the employee does.

5) A <u>salary</u> is a <u>fixed</u> amount paid every <u>month</u> — this doesn't change even if the number of hours worked does change. It is usually paid to <u>office staff</u> who do not directly help to make the product. A salary of £24 000 means you are paid £2000 per month.

6) The advantage of a salary is that the firm and workers both <u>know exactly</u> how much the pay will be. However, it <u>doesn't</u> link pay directly to <u>performance</u>, so it doesn't encourage employees to <u>work harder</u>.

Employers can Give Staff Financial Extras

<u>On top</u> of their regular payments (wage or salary), some firms offer staff <u>extra financial incentives</u> to help to motivate them. For example:

1) <u>Commission</u> — this is paid to sales staff for <u>every item</u> they sell. It is given to them on top of a <u>small basic salary</u>.

> But I only wanted one...

2) <u>Bonus</u> — a <u>lump sum</u> added to pay, usually once a year. It's commonly paid if the worker (or the firm) has met their <u>performance targets</u>.

> BUSINESS EXAMPLE

- <u>John Lewis Partnership</u> is a business that employs around <u>80 000 staff</u>.
- One of the main aims of the business is to keep its employees as <u>happy</u> and <u>motivated</u> as possible.
- Each year, if performance targets are met, John Lewis Partnership gives a <u>proportion</u> of its <u>profits</u> to its employees as a <u>bonus</u>. Each employee gets a <u>percentage</u> of their <u>salary</u>.

3) <u>Fringe benefit</u> — any reward that is not part of a worker's <u>main income</u>. Examples include <u>staff discount</u> on the firm's products, the use of a <u>company car</u>, <u>gym membership</u>, a daily <u>meal allowance</u> or free <u>health insurance</u>. All of these perks <u>cost</u> money for the business, and <u>save</u> it for the worker.

Financial rewards — I'm in it for the money, innit?

Q1 A hotel's rate of pay for a cleaner is higher than that of other local hotels. Explain how this might affect the productivity of the cleaners.

More On Motivation

Now, some <u>more ways</u> that firms try to keep their minions <u>happy</u> and <u>stop</u> them from <u>wandering off</u>. First up is another <u>financial</u> method (promotion), and then three methods that <u>don't</u> involve throwing <u>cash</u> around...

Promotion **Can Boost Motivation**

1) Employees can be <u>trained</u> to learn <u>new skills</u>. This means they can start to take on <u>new tasks</u> and have <u>greater responsibility</u>.

2) This may lead to them getting a <u>promotion</u>, which is likely to mean they get <u>paid more</u>. So <u>promotion</u> (and the <u>opportunity</u> to get promoted) can <u>motivate</u> staff.

A promotion is when an employee is given a higher status or position within a firm.

Job Rotation **Gives Workers a Change** *Now and Again*

1) A lot of production jobs are <u>boring and repetitive</u>, e.g. working on a factory assembly line. <u>Job rotation</u> reduces this by occasionally <u>moving</u> workers from <u>one job to another</u>.

2) This <u>motivates</u> workers as they <u>don't get so bored</u>. They also learn to do <u>different jobs</u>, so if someone's ill, someone else will be able to <u>cover</u>.

3) The problem is that if <u>one</u> boring job is replaced by <u>another</u> it doesn't improve <u>job satisfaction</u>.

Job Enrichment **Gives Workers Better** *Things to Do*

1) <u>Job enrichment</u> is when a worker is given <u>greater responsibility</u> — for example <u>supervising</u> the work of new staff.

2) As a worker becomes <u>good</u> at their job they become <u>more productive</u> — they can do the same work in less time. So, giving workers more responsibility can stop them from feeling that their increased productivity is being <u>punished</u> by more of the same work.

3) It gives workers <u>new challenges</u> and so may <u>motivate</u> them to <u>work harder</u>.

4) A problem is that they may expect a <u>pay rise</u> as well. Some people are never happy...

Autonomy **Gives Workers a Chance to Make Their** *Own Decisions*

1) <u>Autonomy</u> means giving workers the <u>freedom</u> to make their <u>own decisions</u>. Workers may be told their <u>overall goal</u> but not told <u>specifically</u> how they should achieve it.

2) This responsibility <u>motivates</u> workers as it makes them feel <u>trusted</u> and like their contribution is <u>valued</u>.

BUSINESS EXAMPLE

1) Ranbir Singh owns a small chain of <u>hotels</u> in the North of England. Each hotel has a <u>head chef</u> in its restaurant.

2) Ranbir gives each head chef <u>autonomy</u> over the <u>menus</u> in their restaurant. Ranbir decides how <u>profitable</u> the menu should be, but leaves it up to the head chef to decide <u>what dishes</u> go on the menu, <u>where</u> the <u>ingredients</u> will come from, the <u>price</u> of each dish, etc.

Tasty food = auto-nom-nom-nom-y...

Managers have loads of tricks to keep workers motivated and working hard. Make sure you learn all the methods here and on the previous page. Remember, there are five financial methods (remuneration, commission, bonuses, fringe benefits and promotion) and three non-financial methods (job rotation, job enrichment and autonomy).

Case Study — Topic 2.5

Organising, recruiting, training and motivating people — there's a lot to remember in this topic. It's time to apply what you've learnt about human resources to a case study.

Business Report: Making Human Resource Decisions

Lekker Lunch

Lekker Lunch is a rapidly expanding cafe chain. It has recently opened a new branch and recruited all of its ten floor and kitchen staff by advertising on the noticeboards at a local university. It has also recruited a supervisor for the new branch by promoting a member of the floor staff from another branch. The manager of the new branch also manages another two local Lekker Lunch branches. The organisational structure of the business is shown on the right.

Lekker Lunch is employing half of its new floor and kitchen staff on zero hour contracts. The other staff are all employed on a part-time basis.

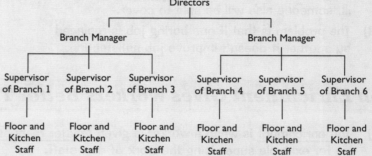

The new staff all received informal training, which was given by the supervisor. After five weeks, the supervisor had a meeting with each part-time employee and set them performance targets. She planned to give each employee a performance review in six months time. The new staff were also given an information pack about Lekker Lunch when they started. This included a brief description of the company and a staff discount card which entitled them to 30% off food at any Lekker Lunch cafe.

Case Study Questions

Think about what you've learnt about human resources to answer these questions.

1) Suggest one reason why Lekker Lunch advertised for its floor and kitchen staff on noticeboards rather than in the local or national press.

2) Suggest why Lekker Lunch chose not to employ any of its floor and kitchen staff on a full-time basis.

3) Give two reasons why a Lekker Lunch employee might be motivated to work for the company.

4) The supervisor in each branch has the authority to make certain decisions without consulting the branch manager. Explain one advantage and one disadvantage of this.

5) Explain how the supervisor's system of monitoring performance may reduce the money Lekker Lunch needs to spend on recruitment.

It's nearly the end of human resources...

I don't mean we're all going to die. I mean you've just got a page of Revision Summary questions to go. Phew.

Revision Summary — Topic 2.5

Whoop-de-woo, the end of another topic. And it wasn't too bad really — just a little bit of how people are organised and kept happy in a business. Here's something that might not keep you happy though — some revision summary questions to make sure you haven't been skim-reading too much...

1) Outline the responsibilities of each of the following job roles:

    a) director,   b) supervisor,   c) support staff.

2) What layer of staff is usually ranked immediately below directors?

3) Which would have more layers of management — a hierarchical or a flat organisational structure?

4) What is the difference between a centralised and a decentralised organisation?

5) Give one advantage of a centralised organisation.

6) Give two disadvantages of a decentralised organisation.

7) List four barriers to communication.

8) Explain why insufficient communication can lead to inefficiency in a firm.

9) Explain why excessive communication can demotivate staff.

10) What does it mean if a staff member is 'full-time'?

11) Describe one way in which a firm may allow an employee to work flexible hours.

12) Explain the difference between a permanent and a temporary contract of employment.

13) What is a freelance contract?

14) Explain why advances in technology have led to more employees working remotely.

15) What is a job description?

16) Give two disadvantages to a firm of filling a vacant position internally rather than externally.

17) Why might a firm prefer candidates to fill in an application form rather than just send in their CV?

18) What does it mean if an employee is encouraged to 'self-learn'?

19) Explain one advantage and one disadvantage of informal training over formal training.

20) Explain how performance reviews can help staff to develop.

21) Explain how motivating staff affects productivity in a business.

22) Give two forms of remuneration that employees may get.

23) What does it mean if a business pays its employees commission?

24) What is meant by a 'fringe benefit'?

25) Give three examples of fringe benefits a firm might offer its employees.

26) How does job rotation help to motivate employees?

27) Explain what is meant by the term 'job enrichment'.

28) Explain why autonomy may help to motivate workers.

The Exams

By now your brain should be full of Business knowledge, ready to impress the examiners. These pages have info and tips on what to expect in the exams, so that you can ace them.

There Are Two Exam Papers — Paper 1 and Paper 2

Paper 1

- Paper 1 is 1 hour and 30 minutes long.
- It's worth 90 marks and is 50% of your total Business GCSE.
- It'll test you on information from Theme 1 — Topics 1.1 to 1.5 of this book.

Paper 2

- Paper 2 is 1 hour and 30 minutes long.
- It's worth 90 marks and is 50% of your total Business GCSE.
- It'll test you on information from Theme 2 — Topics 2.1 to 2.5 of this book.

1) In both papers there'll be three sections.
2) Section A is a mixture of multiple choice, short and long questions. It's worth 35 marks.
3) Sections B and C are both based around a case study, which could include some data. You'll have to answer a mixture of short and long questions related to the information in each case study. Section B is worth 30 marks and Section C is worth 25 marks.

> In this book, you'll find case studies followed by some questions. These case studies may be illustrative examples, or real-life businesses. You don't need to learn the details of these case studies, but you should have a go at answering the questions to help you with Sections B and C in the exams.

The Examiners are Looking for Three Types of Skills

There are basically three types of skill and knowledge that you need to show to get marks in the exams:

Demonstrate knowledge and understanding

- This skill is all about... well... recalling, selecting and communicating.
- You need to show that you've got a really good understanding of the facts, and that you can use appropriate business terms, e.g. sole trader, marketing mix, revenue.

Apply knowledge and understanding

- This skill is all about applying what you know to different situations.
- Make sure your answer is relevant to the situation that's been described.

- For example, an exam question might tell you about a sole trader who wants to buy a new piece of equipment, and ask you to suggest how they could raise the necessary finance. Here, you wouldn't want to suggest that the company issue more shares (since only a limited company can have shares and sole traders are unlimited).

Analyse and evaluate to demonstrate understanding, make judgements and draw conclusions

- This skill is all about using evidence to make judgements and reach conclusions.
- For example, if you recommend that a business raise money using a loan rather than an overdraft, you need to explain why, using what you know about finance.
- Your ideas need to be structured in a logical way so that your arguments make sense.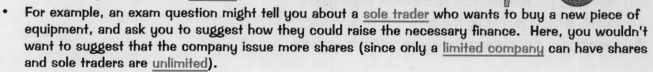
- Often, these questions won't have a right answer. The important thing is using evidence from the question to support the conclusion you've come to.

Survival — that's my exam skill...

So, two exams, 1 hour and 30 minutes each. Simple. Well... maybe 'simple' is a bit strong — they don't give these GCSEs away. But knowing what to expect when you go into your exams can make your life that little bit easier.

Answering Questions

Doing well in Business is made a whole heap easier if you know <u>how</u> to answer the <u>questions</u>...

Make Sure you Read the Question

1) <u>Command words</u> are just the bit of the question that tell you what to do.

2) You'll find answering exam questions much easier if you <u>understand</u> exactly what they <u>mean</u>:

Command word	What to do
State or Give	These words ask for a <u>statement</u> — you don't need to back it up with evidence.
Define	You need to write down <u>what a term means</u>.
Identify	You need to <u>interpret data</u> shown on a <u>graph</u> or in a <u>table</u> to get your answer.
Calculate	Some questions ask for a bit of <u>maths</u>. Remember to <u>show your working</u>.
Complete	You need to <u>fill in</u> the <u>missing parts</u> of some <u>information</u> you've been given (e.g. complete a table).
Outline	You need to make <u>two main points</u> about a business issue and <u>link</u> them together.
Explain	This means you need to give <u>reasons</u> for things. You need to show that you understand how <u>business issues</u> can <u>impact other areas</u> of a business.
Discuss	You should give a <u>long answer</u>, which <u>describes and explains</u> a business issue.
Analyse	This means "Examine in detail." You should talk about the <u>main features</u> of the thing you're analysing. Then explain <u>how</u> these features collectively <u>affect the business</u>.
Justify	You'll be given some information about a business and asked to <u>recommend</u> whether the business should <u>do something</u>, or to choose between <u>two options</u> for what the business could do.
Evaluate	You should discuss and analyse <u>both sides</u> of an issue. You should finish your answer with a <u>conclusion</u> giving an <u>overall judgement</u>.

3) In general, you'll need to <u>spend more time</u> and <u>write more</u> for questions that are worth <u>more marks</u>.

4) Questions with the command words <u>discuss</u>, <u>analyse</u>, <u>justify</u> or <u>evaluate</u> are worth the most — they'll be 6, 9 or 12 marks. For these questions, it might help to write a <u>quick plan</u> to make sure you don't <u>miss anything</u>, and to make sure you show the <u>skills</u> from the previous page.

You'll have to Answer Questions About Case Studies

1) For questions that are based on <u>case study</u> information or on <u>data</u>, make sure you <u>use evidence</u> from the case study or data set <u>as well as</u> your knowledge of Business in your answer.

2) For questions using 'justify' or 'evaluate' command words, there will usually be <u>advantages</u> and <u>disadvantages</u> of a situation to think about — to get all the marks, you'll need to give <u>both sides</u> of the argument before coming to a conclusion.

You'll often have to consider how different parts of a business work together when answering case study questions.

3) Before you get started on your answer, read the <u>case study</u> and any <u>data</u> all the way through.

You'll be Tested on Your Maths Skills

1) Maths is everywhere, and your GCSE Business exams are <u>no exception</u>.

2) You might be asked do some <u>calculations</u> using financial data, or <u>interpret</u> a graph.

3) If you're doing a calculation question, make sure you <u>show your working</u> — even if your final answer's wrong, you could still get some marks if your <u>method</u> was correct.

4) And don't forget to take a <u>calculator</u> to the exams.

Sick of revision yet? Give reasons for your answer...

For each question in the exams, look at the command words and the number of marks. Remember that longer questions are usually testing your judgement as well as your knowledge, so support your ideas with evidence.

Answers

Note on Answers:
A lot of the time in Business, there isn't really a "right answer". Instead, it's about being able to explain yourself and justify your decisions.

Theme 1: Topic 1.2 — Spotting a Business Opportunity

Page 4 — Competition
Q1 E.g. high competition because there's likely to be lots of shops selling clothes on a local high street.

Q2 Any two from: e.g. it could sell its products at a lower price than its competitors. / It could sell its products in a convenient location for customers. / It could offer customer service. / It could increase the size of its product range.

Page 7 — Using Market Research
Q1 a) quantitative
b) qualitative

Page 9 — Case Study — Topics 1.1 & 1.2
Q1 E.g. Ankita has come up with her idea due to changes in what customers want, as more people are cycling, so there will be a greater demand for cycling clothing.

Q2 Hint — think about the things that can be done to add value to a product. Then try and work out which method Ankita has used, and explain why it will add value to her cycling clothing.
E.g. Ankita is planning to develop a strong brand image for her business, which will add value to the cycling clothing as customers will be more willing to spend money on clothing if they recognise the brand and know that it is trustworthy and desirable.

Q3 Hint — think about what market research Ankita has done, and how it may help her when setting up her business.
E.g. Ankita has used market research to map the market. This may help her to discover a gap in the market, and so allow her to develop clothing that is different to her competitors. This will help to increase her sales.

Q4 secondary research

Q5 E.g. Ankita should target people who cycle to commute. From her market research, Ankita has found that the percentage of people cycling to commute has increased over time. Ankita's market map shows that there aren't any businesses making fashion-focused cycling clothing that isn't high performance. So there could be a gap in the market for this type of clothing. From the people Ankita surveyed, she found that the people who only cycle to commute prioritised how fashionable their clothing is, whereas people who race are more interested in it being high performance. So Ankita could take advantage of the gap in the market and target commuters who are likely to be interested in fashionable clothing, and won't mind if it isn't high performance.

Theme 1: Topic 1.3 — Putting a Business Idea into Practice

Page 12 — More on Business Aims and Objectives
Q1 a) E.g. Green Machines could set measurable profit targets each year that it could then work towards achieving.

b) Hint — your answer should include a sensible suggestion of the type of aims that a new firm might have.
E.g. the new firm won't be established in the market, so it may have aims focused on survival, rather than maximising profit.

Page 13 — Revenue, Cost and Profit
Q1 revenue = quantity sold × price = 5000 × 7
= £35 000
profit = revenue − costs = 35 000 − 12 500
= **£22 500**

Page 15 — More on Break-Even Analysis
Q1 2500 − 1300 = **1200 units**

Page 19 — Case Study — Topic 1.3
Q1 E.g. Lizzie may have had an aim to gain the independence of being her own boss so that she could fit her work commitments around her family life.
Lizzie may have had an aim of personal satisfaction by selling handbags that she likes, as she's always had an interest in handbags.

Q2 She may end up losing her money if the business fails.

Q3 E.g. Lizzie may have had an aim to achieve financial security for the business and reach the stage where the business's activities could be paid for using its own revenue. This would have been a good aim because she used her own personal savings to set up the business and has since needed a loan to fund new equipment.

Q4 % interest = (total repayment − borrowed amount) ÷ borrowed amount × 100
= (15 120 − 14 000) ÷ 14 000 × 100
= 1120 ÷ 14 000 × 100 = 0.08 × 100 = **8%**

Q5 Employee salaries = 19 000 × 3 = £57 000
Rent = 1100 × 12 = 13 200
Total fixed costs = 57 000 + 13 200
= **£70 200**

Q6 break-even output in units = fixed cost ÷ (sales price − variable cost)
= 70 200 ÷ (55 − 15) = 70 200 ÷ 40
= **1755 units**

Q7 The break-even output will increase because the loan repayments will have increased Lizzie's fixed costs.

Theme 1: Topic 1.4 — Making the Business Effective

Page 21 — Business Ownership Structures
Q1 E.g. having her brother as a partner means he could put capital into the business, meaning it could grow faster. However, Jennifer would have to share the profits of the business with her brother, so she could end up with less money for herself.

Page 24 — The Marketing Mix
Q1 Hint — you have to think about the impact of the new type of product on both of the elements of the marketing mix in the question.
E.g. the business is likely to give its new cheese a high price since it is of high quality and so will probably use more expensive ingredients. The business is likely to emphasise the quality of the new cheese in its promotion in order to attract customers.

Page 27 — Case Study — Topic 1.4
Q1 E.g. setting up as a sole trader is easy so Sophie can start her business straight away. / Setting up as a sole trader means Sophie is her own boss so she doesn't have to get anyone else's agreement to make decisions.

Q2 E.g. Sophie should print out flyers because her business is new and flyers are a much cheaper way to promote her business than a TV advert. Also, if she gives out flyers in the area around her shop, they are more likely to reach her potential customers than a TV advert.

Q3 E.g. the bank may agree to give her a loan because she has produced a business plan, which will give the bank details about how the business will operate and so how the bank will get its money back.

The bank may not agree to give her a loan because she is a sole trader and so a high risk option for a bank to loan to. This is because, if the business fails, the bank could lose all the money that it has given to Sophie.

Q4 Hint — for whichever site you choose, you need to justify why this site would be better than the other two using information from the case study. Make sure you discuss the effects of factors such as location of the market and competition. It doesn't matter which location you choose, as long as you are able to justify your answer.
E.g. Sophie should choose 12 Market Street. This is a popular area, so the market is likely to be larger than Sutcliff Park and a similar size to Mega Mall. Even though 12 Market Street is more expensive than Sutcliff Park, having a larger market means that the café should sell more, which should cover the extra cost. There is some competition on the street from other cafés, but none of these cafés sell ice cream, so Sophie will still have a unique selling point. At Mega Mall, the shop would be surrounded by other food outlets. This could be good, as people will come to the area for food, but the competition also means some of these people will use the other cafés. At the park, there is no competition in the winter, but during the summer an ice cream van will be in direct competition with the café. As summer is likely to be the busiest period for the café, it could have a big impact on Sophie's sales.

Theme 1: Topic 1.5 — Understanding External Influences on Business

Page 33 — Consumer Law
Q1 E.g. the product is not fit for purpose as it can't be used to store normal pens / the product doesn't match its description, which said it was suitable for standard stationery needs.

Page 35 — Inflation and Consumer Income
Q1 Hint — for both part a) and b), you need to explain the effect on the business, not just describe what might happen.

a) E.g. George is likely to see an increase in sales. This is because people will be spending a smaller proportion of their income on things that they need than before, so they'll have more to spend on luxuries such as eating at restaurants. This means demand for George's restaurant is likely to go up.

b) E.g. George's sales are likely to go down. This is because people will be spending more of their income on things that they need than before, so they'll have less to spend on luxuries such as dining out at restaurants. So demand for George's restaurant is likely to go down.

Page 38 — Case Study — Topic 1.5
Q1 E.g. having a website would have meant that Frame the Wall Ltd. could reach a wider market, so they would have got sales from new customers outside of their local area.

Q2 E.g. they must not discriminate against anyone because of their religion, gender, race, age, sexual orientation or because of disabilities. They must also make sure that any new recruit has a legal right to work in the UK.

Q3 a) E.g. the employees are likely to have been in favour of the plans to reinvest a large percentage of the profit, because if the company grew successfully they may have had more job security and may have been able to get a promotion.

b) E.g. some shareholders may not have been in favour of the plans to reinvest a large percentage of the profit, as it was likely to mean that they got lower dividends in the short-term.

Q4 Hint — Make sure you consider each of the four factors mentioned in the table. For each one, explain how it could affect the money Frame the Wall Ltd. would have available for growth.

The amount of tax that the business had to pay on its profits was expected to fall significantly. This means that Frame the Wall Ltd. would have been able to keep more of their profits, so they would have had more money available to reinvest.

Inflation was expected to fall from its high level. This could have been beneficial for the firm as it suggests that their costs would not rise much in the following years. This means that Frame the Wall Ltd. would have made more profit on their sales, meaning they would have more money to reinvest.

Consumer incomes were expected to rise at a faster rate than inflation. This may have been beneficial to Frame the Wall Ltd. as people would have had more money to spend on luxuries, which may have led to an increase in demand for their products. Expecting demand for their products to grow may have given Frame the Wall Ltd. more confidence that they could survive if they grew the business.

Interest rates were expected to rise from their low level. This could have meant that the firm had less money available for investment as it would have to pay back more on any money it had borrowed. Also consumers may have had less money available to spend as they would also need to pay back more on money they had borrowed, meaning that demand for their products may have fallen. However, interest rates were only expected to rise slightly so Frame the Wall Ltd. may not have been too worried about these impacts.

Theme 2: Topic 2.1 — Growing the Business

Page 41 — More on Business Growth

Q1 a) E.g. the law of increased dimensions means that, even though the factory is double the size, it doesn't cost twice as much to operate it. This means that the average cost of producing each board game will fall.

b) Expanding will lead to economies of scale, meaning that the average unit cost will fall. This means that Lucky Dice can afford to charge less for their games and still make a profit.

c) Hint — you should state one problem that Lucky Dice might experience from being bigger, and explain how it will affect the business.
E.g. Lucky Dice have hired more staff. Having more staff means it will be harder to communicate within the company. This could cause the employees to become demotivated and productivity to go down.

Page 44 — Globalisation

Q1 E.g. Pillow Perfect could use e-commerce to sell pillow cases to customers in foreign countries. Pillow Perfect could also change its marketing mix so its products appeal to customers from other countries.

Page 47 — Case Study — Topic 2.1

Q1 2010, because by this time Coca-Cola® had (18 + 38) 56% shares in innocent drinks. A company can take over another company once it owns more than 50% of the shares.

Q2 E.g. the money doesn't have to be repaid.

Q3 A multinational company is a single business operating in more than one country, so they will have access to supply chains in other countries and potential new markets there.

Q4 In 2003 and 2007, innocent drinks targeted new markets by setting up branches in other European countries. In 2013, innocent drinks developed new products by launching noodle pots, kids' fruity water and extra juicy smoothies.

Q5 It means that the company works in ways that won't damage the Earth for future generations.

Q6 Hint — make sure you talk about both the possible positive and negative impacts to innocent drinks of its sustainable and ethical practices.
E.g. innocent drinks' sustainable and ethical practices may attract more customers who are concerned about environmental and ethical issues, which could increase profit over time. However, innocent drinks is likely to have experienced higher costs due to these practices. For example, it may have had to spend money on changing to new equipment and processes that meet sustainability standards and waste less energy. These increased costs may mean that innocent drinks makes less profit on each item that it sells. It could increase the price of its products to avoid a fall in profit, but this may lead to a loss of custom, which would lead to lower revenue and lower profits.
Due to its ethical policies, innocent drinks donates 10% of its profits each year to charity, which means it has less profit to reinvest in the business.

Theme 2: Topic 2.2 — Making Marketing Decisions

Page 49 — The Marketing Mix and The Design Mix

Q1 Hint — there are three elements to the design mix, so make sure you describe how the business should consider each one for its new cat food product.
E.g. the business should make sure that the new product fulfils its function as an appropriate source of food for cats, the manufacturing costs should be kept low, and the packaging should be attractive to customers.

Page 53 — Pricing Strategies

Q1 E.g. the supermarket is using a loss leader pricing strategy. It might be using this strategy so that customers come into the store to buy a steak pie and then also buy other, profitable products while they are there.

Page 56 — Case Study — Topic 2.2

Q1 E.g. the cereal market is very competitive which means that if Nestlé® charges too much for its products compared to its competitors then customers may buy other cereal products. Therefore its cereals are likely to be priced at a similar level to other products in the market in order to stay competitive.

Q2 E.g. sales of breakfast cereals are falling, so Nestlé® might have chosen to advertise Shreddies in order to remind people about the product, which may increase sales/extend the life of the product.

Q3 Hint — Talk about the pros and cons of producing television adverts and how appropriate this method was for Nestlé®. Use information from the case study to analyse the success of the advert and explain how this success is likely to have affected sales.
E.g. although television adverts are expensive, they are seen by a wide audience and can deliver long messages. This method of advertising was appropriate for Nestle® as they are a big company that can afford the advertising costs. Breakfast cereals are eaten by many different types of people across the country, so using TV adverts is a good way for Nestlé® to target a wide audience. The adverts were very popular and Nestlé® went on to develop a successful Facebook® page using the Knitting Nana characters. The Facebook® page will have continued to promote the brand, with over 250 000 people being fans of the site. The Knitting Nanas are likely to have created lots of positive awareness of the brand, meaning that people would be more tempted to buy it, so sales are likely to have increased.

Q4 E.g. Nestlé® have differentiated Shreddies Max by giving it a unique selling point, as it is labelled as being a good source of protein. This will make Shreddies Max seem different to the other cereals on the market, which should make customers want to buy it, rather than another cereal brand. This should increase sales for Nestlé®.

Q5 E.g. the demand for Shreddies Max is likely to have been low at first, since the product was only in the introduction phase of its life cycle. However, demand may have increased as the product is likely to have entered its growth phase during this time. Since there were not many other cereals on the market labelled as high protein, customers wanting a high protein cereal wouldn't have much choice, so would have been more likely to buy Shreddies Max.

Theme 2: Topic 2.3 — Making Operational Decisions

Page 58 — Methods of Production

Q1 a) job production

b) E.g. products made by job production are expensive so the theatre company may not have been able to afford to have all of the costumes made by Which Stitch. Job production can take a long time so there may not have been enough time for Which Stitch to make all of the costumes before the play.

Page 62 — Quality

Q1 E.g. a quality control system should mean that the events Partee Maxx puts on are all good quality. So the business may get known for providing a high quality service, which could improve its brand image. This may give Partee Maxx a competitive advantage as customers may be more likely to use them, rather than competing firms.

Theme 2: Topic 2.4 — Making Financial Decisions

Page 65 — Business Calculations

Q1 Total profit = 26 − 14 = £12m
Average annual profit = 12m ÷ 3 years = £4m
ARR = (average annual profit ÷ cost of investment) × 100
= (4 ÷ 14) × 100 = **28.6%** (1 d.p.)

Page 66 — More on Business Calculations

Q1 gross profit = revenue − cost of sales
= 200 000 − 40 000 = £160 000
gross profit margin = (gross profit ÷ revenue) × 100
= (160 000 ÷ 200 000) × 100
= 0.8 × 100 = **80%**

Page 68 — Case Study — Topics 2.3 & 2.4

Q1 E.g. Marks and Spencer makes sure that its suppliers provide it with products that are high quality. This means Marks and Spencer should get a reputation for supplying high quality products to its customers. This will help to make it more competitive against firms whose suppliers provide lower quality goods.

Q2 gross profit margin = gross profit ÷ sales × 100
= (3817.4 m ÷ 9222.1 m) × 100 = **41.4%** (1 d.p.)

Q3 The batch cards make sure employees check their own work and that employees pass on good quality work to the next stage in the production process. This should help stop errors from being made in the first place, rather than having to get rid of faulty goods once they have been made.

Q4 Batch production will allow the factories to make batches of clothes in different colours/sizes/styles, and then stop, reorganise and make a batch of something else. This is suitable because all the clothes within one batch will be identical, so using batch production means the factory will be more productive and can take advantage of economies of scale. However, it also means the factory will be able to adapt and make many different types of clothes.

Q5 Using just-in-time means that stock levels are kept low. This means that the costs of the factories should be lower, as they won't need to store lots of stock, and they should have less waste. As the factories' costs will be lower, they are likely to charge Marks and Spencer less for each item of clothing, which in turn will reduce Marks and Spencer's cost of sales. This will lead to their gross profit margin increasing.

Theme 2: Topic 2.5 — Making Human Resource Decisions

Page 70 — Internal Organisational Structures

Q1 E.g. there are more layers of management in a hierarchical structure, which could make communication in KS Dentistry Ltd. difficult/slow because more people need to pass on the message.

Page 74 — Recruitment

Q1 a) A document which lists the qualifications, experience, skills and attitudes a person needs to have for a particular job.

b) Any two from: e.g. it is cheaper. / The post can be filled more quickly. / The new recruit will already know a lot about the firm. / The bosses may already know the candidate well.

Page 76 — Motivation

Q1 It might increase their productivity, as the cleaners will feel more motivated to work for the hotel. They will want the hotel to be successful, so they will do their jobs well to help this happen.

Page 78 — Case Study — Topic 2.5

Q1 E.g. it's much cheaper to advertise on noticeboards than it is to advertise in the local or national press.

Q2 E.g. it may not be worth paying for full-time staff as the cafe is only likely to get busy during certain periods.

Q3 Any two from: e.g. they will get paid for the work they do. / They get 30% off food at any Lekker Lunch cafe. / There is a possibility of promotion within the company.

Q4 E.g. an advantage is that less communication is needed within the business, so changes can be made more quickly / this additional responsibility may make the supervisor feel more valued in the business and therefore more motivated. A disadvantage is that inconsistencies may develop between the different branches as each supervisor will make different decisions.

Q5 Hint — In your answer you should explain how performance reviews help to motivate staff and how this in turn can lead to higher levels of staff retention.
E.g. having performance targets and performance reviews may make the employees feel more motivated because if they meet their performance targets they might be rewarded. Knowing that their supervisor is interested in how well they are doing their job and is willing to help them to develop may also motivate the employees. Motivated staff are more likely to stay with the firm, so the system of monitoring performance is likely to increase Lekker Lunch's level of staff retention. This means they will not have to replace staff members as often, so their recruitment costs may fall.

Glossary

advertising	Any message that a firm pays for, which promotes the firm or its products.
aim	An overall goal that a business is trying to achieve.
ARR	The average rate of return on an investment.
asset	A valuable item owned by a business, or money owed to the business.
autonomy	Where a worker is given the freedom to make their own decisions in their job.
bar gate stock graph	A graph that is used to manage a business's stock levels.
batch production	A method of production in which a firm makes one batch of identical items at a time.
bonus	A lump sum added to an employee's pay, usually once a year.
brand image	The impression that customers have of a company or the products it sells.
break-even level of output	The level of output at which a company's total revenue equals its total costs.
business enterprise	The process of identifying new business opportunities, and then taking advantage of them.
business plan	An outline of what a business will do and how it aims to do it.
cash	The money a business can spend immediately.
cash flow	The flow of all money into and out of a business.
cash inflow	Money that flows into a business.
cash outflow	Money that flows out of a business.
centralised organisation	An organisation in which all major decisions are made by one person or a few senior managers at the top of the organisational structure.
commission	Money paid to sales staff for every item they sell on top of their basic salary.

competitor	A business which sells the same products in the same market as another business.
consumer	The person who uses a good or service.
cost	An expense paid out to run a business.
crowd funding	When a large number of people each contribute money towards funding a new business or a business idea.
customer service	Any interaction a business has with its customers.
CV (curriculum vitae)	A summary of a person's personal details, skills, qualifications and interests.
decentralised organisation	An organisation in which the authority to make most decisions is shared between people at different layers of the organisational structure.
demand	How much of a product or service people will be willing to buy at a given price.
design mix	The different elements of design needed to make a product successful, including its function, cost and aesthetics.
differentiation	Making products or services distinctive in the market.
diseconomy of scale	Where growth can lead to an increase in average unit cost.
dividend	A payment that a shareholder gets if the company makes a profit.
e-commerce	Buying and selling products on the internet.
e-tailer	A company that sells products online.
economy of scale	A reduction in average unit cost that comes from producing on a large scale.
entrepreneur	Someone who takes on the risks of enterprise activity.
exchange rate	A value that tells you how much one unit of a currency costs in a different currency.
extension strategy	An action intended to extend the life of a product.
external (inorganic) growth	When a company grows by merging with or taking over another firm.
external recruitment	Where a business recruits new people from outside the business.
fixed cost	A cost that does not vary with output.
flat structure	An organisational structure with very few layers.
flexible working	When working hours and patterns are adapted to suit the employee.
flow production	A method of production in which all products are identical and are made as quickly as possible.
formal training	A method of training which has a set plan with learning objectives and a schedule.
franchise	Where a company lets another firm sell its products or use its trademarks in return for a fee or a percentage of the profits.
freelance contract	When a self-employed person is recruited by a company on a temporary basis, usually to work on a specific project.
fringe benefit	Any reward for an employee that is not part of their regular income.
full-time staff	Employees that generally work 35-40 hours a week.

gap in the market	A customer need that isn't being met.
globalisation	The process by which businesses and countries around the world become more connected.
gross profit	The profit left over once the cost of sales has been taken away from the total revenue.
gross profit margin	The fraction of every pound spent by customers that doesn't go towards making the product.
hierarchical structure	An organisational structure with lots of layers.
incorporated	A business that has its own legal identity.
inflation	An increase in the price of goods and services.
informal training	A method of training which has no strict plan and is usually given by other workers.
insolvency	When a firm is unable to pay its debts.
interest rate	A value which shows the cost of borrowing money or the reward given for saving money.
internal (organic) growth	When a company grows by expanding its own activities.
internal recruitment	Where existing employees are recruited into new roles within a business.
job description	A written description of what a job involves.
job enrichment	Where a worker is given greater responsibility in their job.
job production	A method of production in which each product has a unique design based on the customer's specification.
job rotation	Where a worker is occasionally moved from one job to another.
just-in-time (JIT)	A method used in production or stock management in which stock levels are kept at a bare minimum — products are made just in time for delivery to customers.
limited liability	Where the owners of a business are not legally responsible for all the debts a business has.
loan	A long-term source of money that must be paid back to the lender.
logistics	Getting goods or services from one part of the supply chain to another.
margin of safety	The gap between current level of output and the break-even level of output.
market	A place where goods are traded between customers and suppliers, trade in a particular type of product or the potential customers for a product.
market map	A diagram showing some of the features of a market.
market research	Investigation of the features of a market and customer opinions within the market.
market share	The proportion of total sales within a market that is controlled by a business.
market size	The number of individuals (including companies) within a market that are potential buyers and sellers of products, or the total value of products in the market.
marketing mix	The four elements that must be considered for good marketing: product, price, promotion and place.
mass market	A large group of potential customers for a product.
merger	When two companies join together to form a new, larger firm.
multinational	A single business that operates in more than one country.

net profit	The profit left over when all costs are taken into account.
net profit margin	The fraction of every pound spent by customers that the company gets to keep.
niche market	A small and specialised group of potential customers for a product.
objective	A measurable step that a business will set in order to work towards an aim.
obsolete	When a product is no longer used, usually because it has become out-dated and has been replaced by something else.
overdraft	When more money is taken out of a bank account than has been paid into it.
part-time staff	Employees that generally work 10-30 hours a week.
partnership	A business ownership structure in which a small number of people (usually between 2 and 20) own an unincorporated company.
performance review	A system for assessing an employee's progress and helping them to develop.
permanent contract	A contract of employment that has no end date.
person specification	A list of the qualifications, experience, skills and attitudes a person needs for a particular job.
pressure group	An organisation that tries to influence what people think about a certain subject.
primary research	Market research that involves getting information from customers or potential customers.
private limited company	A business ownership structure that is incorporated and has shares, but the shares can only be sold with the agreement of all the shareholders.
procurement	The act of finding and buying things that a business needs from outside of the business.
product life cycle	The different stages that a product goes through over time.
productivity	How many products are made in a certain amount of time or for a certain amount of money.
profit	The difference between revenue and costs over a period of time.
promotion	When an employee is given a higher status or position within a firm.
public limited company	A business ownership structure that is incorporated and has shares that can be bought and sold by anyone.
qualitative information	Information that involves people's feelings or opinions.
quality assurance	A way of maintaining quality by checking that quality standards are being met throughout each process involved in making a product.
quality control	A way of maintaining quality by checking products for faults at certain stages during the production process.
quantitative information	Information that can be measured or reduced to a number.
remote working	When an employee works in a location away from their employer's offices, e.g. at home.
remuneration	Payment to an employee for the work they have done for an employer.
retailer	A business that sells products to consumers.
retained profit	Profit that is put back into the business.
revenue	The value of all products sold in a given time period.

salary	A fixed payment that is made to employees every month.
sales process	The method by which a business sells items to its customers.
secondary research	Market research that involves looking at data from outside the business, e.g. market reports.
segmentation	When people within a market are divided into different groups.
self-learning	Where an employee seeks out their own training and development.
share	A unit of ownership in a company. Owners of shares can share in the profits of the company.
share capital	Money gained through issuing shares in the company.
sole trader	A business ownership structure where one person owns an unincorporated company.
sponsorship	A method of promotion in which a business gives money to an organisation or event. In return the organisation or event displays the business's name.
staff retention	When a business keeps its staff.
stakeholder	Any individual or group of people that is affected by a business.
stock market	A market where shares of public limited companies can be bought and sold.
sustainability	Working in a way that doesn't damage the Earth for future generations.
takeover	When an existing business expands by buying more than half the shares in another firm.
tariff	A tax on goods that are being imported or exported.
temporary contract	A contract of employment that is only for a fixed period of time.
total cost	The fixed and variable costs for a business added together.
trade bloc	A group of countries that has few or no trade barriers between them.
trade credit	When a businesses give firms time to pay for certain purchases.
unincorporated	A business that doesn't have its own legal identity.
unique selling point (USP)	This is some feature that makes a product different from its competitors.
unlimited liability	Where the owners of a business are legally responsible for all the debts a business has.
variable cost	A cost that will increase as a firm expands output.
venture capital	Money raised through selling shares to individuals or businesses who specialise in giving finance to new or expanding small firms.
viral advertising	When adverts are shared and viewed many (perhaps millions of) times in a short time period, often via social media.
wage	Payment that is usually made to employees weekly or monthly.
zero hour contract	A contract of employment which means the employer doesn't have to offer the employee any work at all and the employee doesn't have to accept any work that is offered to them.

Glossary

Index

Index